UNIVERSITY OF NORTH CAROLINA
STUDIES IN THE ROMANCE LANGUAGES AND LITERATURES
Number 80

THE MYTH OF PARAGUAY
IN THE FICTION OF AUGUSTO ROA BASTOS

THE MYTH OF PARAGUAY
IN THE FICTION OF AUGUSTO ROA BASTOS

BY

DAVID WILLIAM FOSTER

CHAPEL HILL

THE UNIVERSITY OF NORTH CAROLINA PRESS

Published with aid from the Grants Committee,
ARIZONA STATE UNIVERSITY

DEPÓSITO LEGAL: V. 2.924 - 1969

ARTES GRÁFICAS SOLER, S. A. - JÁVEA, 30 - VALENCIA (8) - 1969

CONTENTS

	Page
PREFACE	11

PART ONE. *El trueno entre las hojas:* Seventeen Literary Experiments in the Definition of a People ... 17

INTRODUCTION ... 17
1. "Carpincheros" — The Setting of *El trueno entre las hojas*. 18
2. Stories of Human Suffering ... 23
3. Stories of the Evil in Children ... 27
4. Stories of Human Will ... 30
5. Stories of Human Sacrifice: Adults ... 35
6. Stories of Human Sacrifice: Children ... 39
7. Stories of "Man Crucified by Man" ... 44
CONCLUSION ... 50

PART TWO. *Hijo de hombre:* The Crucifixion and Universal Suffering of Mankind ... 53

INTRODUCTION ... 53
1. The *Cristo de Itapé* as a Symbol ... 57
2. Alexis Dubrovsky — The Misconception of a Symbol ... 64
3. Cristóbal Jara — The Realization of a Symbol ... 68
4. "Ex combatientes" — The Legacy of a Symbol ... 81

CONCLUSION ... 86

*To Virginia,
in memory of Maipú and Paraguay*

PREFACE

Augusto Roa Bastos is without a doubt the most important figure in contemporary Paraguayan literature. As a writer of prose fiction, he represents both a mature realization of that genre in a Paraguay long without novelists of note, as well as the participation of his country's literature, through his own works, in the mainstream of Latin-American literature. [1]

Born in 1917 [2] in Asunción, Roa attended the capital's Colegio San José. The beginnings of his literary vocation are dedicated to poetry, and in 1936 his first book of poems appeared, *El ruiseñor de la aurora y otros poemas*. As Rodríguez Alcalá has observed, Roa Bastos' poetry belongs first to the Renaissance and Baroque traditions of Spanish poetry, and later, with the awakening of a new sensibility, to the poetry of Valle-Inclán, Juan Ramón Jiménez and García Lorca. [3] The poet's most recent selection, *El*

---

[1] In his monumental index of Latin-American literature, Enrique Anderson Imbert finds the opportunity to include only fifty-two Paraguayans out of a total of 2505 authors represented in the indexes of the two volumes; or, in other words, only 2.08 percent of the Latin-American men of letters considered are Paraguayans. Of these fifty-two, thirty-five (67 percent) are still living (as of 1961) and twenty-nine (56 percent) were born in this century. Only seventeen (including Roa Bastos) are listed as writers of prose fiction (33 percent), as opposed to twenty-eight (54 percent) listed as poets (four are listed as essayists, two as chroniclers). Anderson Imbert is able to say categorically at one point: "*Paraguay. No tuvo modernistas porque, en verdad, no tuvo literatura*" (v. 1, p. 397). Enrique Anderson Imbert, *Historia de la literatura hispanoamericana*, 3.ª ed. (México, Fondo de Cultura Económica, 1961).

[2] Some cite 1918 as his birthdate. We accept the authority of the publisher, Editorial Losada.

[3] Hugo Rodríguez Alcalá, "Augusto Roa Bastos y *El trueno entre las*

naranjal ardiente, with the exception of one *memorial,* represents a production terminated in 1949. Roa's efforts are now directed toward the prose narrative, an examination of which is our interest here.[4] At present, Roa resides and works in Buenos Aires.

In her article with Miguel Ángel Fernández, "Aspectos de la cultura paraguaya,"[5] the Paraguayan poetess Josefina Pla affirms that:

> Con *La babosa* [de Gabriel Casaccia (1951)] y las dos obras de Roa Bastos [*El trueno entre las hojas* (1953) e *Hijo de hombre* (1960)], la narrativa paraguaya alcanza por fin nivel continental, salvando con botas de siete leguas un retraso de medio siglo (p. 84).

The implication here, as is demonstrated elsewhere in the article, is that Paraguay has had a paucity of writers of prose narrative. If such is indeed the case, the wide recognition accorded to Roa Bastos is a noteworthy event for Paraguayan letters. However, of a much more central importance is the mature and studied examination of his people and their national identification. Miss Pla, in the same article, comments that:

> Como en los cantos [*El trueno...*], en la novela [*Hijo...*] el lector se transporta a la frontera donde sobre la verdad y aun sobre la verosimilitud de los hechos predomina, como el autor mismo lo ha dicho, "el encantamiento de esos mismos hechos". Sin embargo, el personaje de Roa no deja de ser carne y hueso, con sus íntimas contradicciones que lo aproximan a nuestra sensibilidad, tanto como a nuestra imaginación soliviantada. El dolor que se quiso proscribir está ahí patente, envenenando el aire. Roa —y con él la narrativa paraguaya— se compromete hasta la médula con este dolor de un pueblo y lo hace sentir como porción indivisa del lote universal (p. 84).

---

hojas," *Revista iberoamericana,* XX, No. 39 (1955), 19-45; also in his *Korn, Romero, Güiraldes, Unamuno, Ortega, literatura paraguaya y otros ensayos* (México, Studium, 1958), 171-98.

[4] Roa Bastos has several unedited works, among them, an unfinished novel, two short novels, and a drama.

[5] Josefina Pla and Miguel Ángel Fernández, "Aspectos de la cultura paraguaya," *Cuadernos americanos,* CXX (1962), 68-103.

Roa Bastos is willing to recognize the specific limitations of his narrative perspective. However, commenting upon *Hijo de hombre*,[6] he is quick to affirm that his work possesses a pertinency beyond Paraguay's national boundaries:

> No he pretendido hacer una novela regional o americanista, en el mal sentido del término. No me interesan el color local ni el pintoresquismo, como tampoco las ingenuas premisas de las novelas de tesis o que se proponen una praxis determinista. Si ello ocurre, debe radicar de la temperatura natural del contexto. Sé que nadie puede lograrla premeditadamente, por la sola fuerza de su pensamiento. Ya se ha generalizado y arraigado la convicción de que el novelista debe ser un testigo de su época y sus novelas un testimonio, un acto de participación, el más intenso posible, en la vida intelectual y espiritual de sus semejantes. Ello no está dado por la integridad estética, únicamente: emana sobre todo de su pasión moral, de su espíritu de responsabilidad.
>
> En *Hijo de hombre* he tratado de encontrar uno de los muchos y cambiantes rostros de la verdad de nuestro tiempo, el hombre de todos los tiempos, en la raíz misma de la colectividad a que pertenezco, en la pulsación vital de sus luchas y sacrificios; de esa verdad que, como lo dice Faulkner, el hombre no puede violar sin remordimiento. Y menos, el escritor que debe testimoniar sobre ella (p. 10).

Roa Bastos' two works examined in this study represent but the beginnings of a promising career. Of interest, therefore, are those elements that represent the Paraguayan's potential as an important literary figure. In his article, "El fuego en las manos,"[7] Roa outlines the principles that guide his concept of the office of the novelist, an office which he sees as a mission:

> El hombre de letras contemporáneo siente que su oficio se le torna de más en más una misión, una manera de actuar sobre su contorno, siempre que lo haga dentro

---

[6] Augusto Roa Bastos, "Roa Bastos nos habla de su novela," *Gaceta literaria de Losada* (September, 1960), 10.

[7] Augusto Roa Bastos, "El fuego en las manos," *Diálogo*, 2.ª época, No. 1 (April, 1960), 17-18.

> de los límites propios de su condición y función de escritor. Sumergido en el caldeado debate de nuestro tiempo, no puede evadirlo pero tampoco reflejarlo como un espectador pasivo o como un testigo desinteresado. La disyuntiva es rigurosa: toma en sus manos el candente material y trabaja con él, a la escala de los intereses y de las aspiraciones de su época, de su colectividad; o lo rehuye. Pero en este caso, es casi seguro que su obra resultará inocua. Carecerá de peso específico, de radiación vital y espiritual. La posibilidad de resonancia de un escritor radica sin duda en la autenticidad de su labor, que deviene accesible a la comprensión y emoción de sus contemporáneos porque lleva en sí la semilla de las necesidades, la modulación de sus temas y las respuestas a sus preguntas fundamentales, el aire y la ley del tiempo en que se forjan (p. 17).

Roa Bastos, then, sees his mission as that of representing the vital reality of his own time, of confronting and handling maturely the human problems of the context, both social and temporal, in which he lives. The novelist can no longer be content with the role of chronicler, but must assume a moral and ethical position in relation to the material with which he is working. In short, he must be *engagé*. By adopting such a position the author is called upon to refine the perspective of his immediate reality. Roa Bastos, being Paraguayan, is particularly concerned with the reality of his own people:

> En el caso de la literatura de mi país, puedo decir que los escritores y poetas paraguayos han definido rotundamente su actitud al asociar su obra a las luchas de su pueblo y expresar con ella sus anhelos más intensos. Por caminos dispares, con vibraciones y fisonomías, unos y otros coinciden en colocar su trabajo denodadamente y sin concesiones, en el vórtice de las necesidades y aspiraciones de su colectividad, que es como decir sobre su foco mismo de emoción y energía (pp. 17-18).

It is true that Roa so far has not attempted to take the themes of his works beyond an immediate national level. Paraguay's problems are universal to the extent that they reflect the predominant condition of man and his eternal struggle for the total identification and realization of his personality. Roa Bastos' literary "theory," if it may be so called, is a serious imperative to the novelist to bring his art and the perception that it implies to the examination and analysis of the problems of man and mankind:

> La literatura paraguaya de hoy se forja en un tiempo de rebeldía y anunciación. Se escribe con el pulso y con la sangre. Abrazados estrechamente con su época y con su pueblo, apoyados en la unidad de América en la cultura, los escritores paraguayos de hoy producen sus obras como esos actos de coraje, de patriotismo y de sinceridad, de que hablaba Alberdi. Pasión, coraje y esperanza son sus armas contra la desesperación y la incertidumbre.
>
> Toman resueltamente el fuego en sus manos y alumbran con él los días oscuros y aciagos. Saben que no pueden restar su esfuerzo al movimiento emancipador de su pueblo. Y de estos sentimientos abandonados en la fraternidad, en la fuerza y verdad de su causa, es de donde sacan su clarividencia de artistas, la posibilidad de acertar con la gran ley bajo cuyo signo, en el dominio del mundo y del hombre, la necesidad se aúna con la libertad (p. 18).

It is a recognition of this mature concept of the function of the novelist in a rapidly changing society that is "coming of age" after so many years of bitter oblivion which has led us to undertake an analysis of Roa Bastos' fiction and to consider it as being at this time a propitious and opportune study.

SEMBRADA entre sus vientos capitales
y desde el pecho casi sin orilla,
su corazón estalla en la semilla
de corazones rojos e inmortales.

Al norte, sus cornisas minerales;
la arena, al Oeste, que en los huesos brilla,
y entre el Este y el Sur, la verde quilla
de su barco de tierra y vegetales.

Hundida hasta la frente con su carga
de escombros y de vivos corazones,
mira pasar el tiempo en una larga

sucesión de esperanzas y moñones,
hasta que rompa su prisión amarga
el puño popular de sus varones.

("La tierra," from *El naranjal ardiente*,[8] p. 9)

TAN tierra son los hombres de mi tierra
que ya parece que estuvieran muertos;
por fuera dormidos y despiertos
por dentro con el sueño de la guerra.

Tan tierra son que son ellos la tierra
andando con los huesos de sus muertos,
y no hay semblantes, años ni desiertos
que no muestren el paso de la guerra.

De florecer antiguas cicatrices
tienen la piel arada y su barbecho
alumbran desde el fondo las raíces.

Tan hombres son los hombres de mi tierra
que en el color sangriento de su pecho
la paz florida brota de su guerra.

("Los hombres," from *El naranjal ardiente*, p. 10)

---

[8] Augusto Roa Bastos, *El naranjal ardiente* (Asunción, Cuadernos de la Piririta, 1960).

PART ONE

EL TRUENO ENTRE LAS HOJAS: SEVENTEEN LITERARY EXPERIMENTS IN THE DEFINITION OF A PEOPLE

INTRODUCTION

Roa Bastos' literary production may be divided into two genre types: the poetry of his earlier years (a genre set aside in 1947) [1] and the prose fiction of the most recent years of his literary career. Although Roa makes a complete break with poetry before turning to the short narrative, the extensive and rich experience of the neo-Baroque style that forms the background of his poems carries over into the first extensive attempts at prose fiction, *El trueno entre las hojas*. [2] Without a doubt, the selections, while possessing little common narrative denominator, reveal a common

---

[1] For a discussion of the poetry of Roa Bastos and the poetic antecedents, as well as the poetic characteristics of *El trueno entre las hojas*, see Hugo Rodríguez Alcalá, "Augusto Roa Bastos y *El trueno entre las hojas*," *Revista iberoamericana*, XX, No. 39 (1955), 19-45; also in his *Korn, Romero, Güiraldes, Unamuno, Ortega, literatura paraguaya y otros ensayos* (México, Studium, 1958), 171-98. An exchange between Alcalá and Roa concerning the latter's poetry is to be found in the pages of *El país* (of which Roa was a staff member), September 3, 1938. Alcala's commentary was entitled "Epístola a un poeta de estilo arcaico." Roa responded with "Contestando a una epístola." A selection of Roa's poetry is to be found in the introductory anthology of Sinforiano Buzó-Gómez, *Indice de la poesía paraguaya* (Buenos Aires, Tupá, 1943). For a discussion of Roa in terms of contemporary Paraguayan poetry, as well as further references, see Hugo Rodríguez Alcalá, "Sobre la poesía paraguaya de los últimos veinte años," in his *Korn, Romero...*, cited above, pp. 199-211.

[2] Augusto Roa Bastos, *El trueno entre las hojas*, 2.ª ed. (Buenos Aires, Losada, 1961). Originally published by the same house in 1953.

artistic denominator. The stories are best seen as impressionistic units in which Roa Bastos shows himself an able craftsman with poetic effects, the execution of setting, the impressive interplay of antithetical elements such as light and darkness, silence and sound, passiveness and violence, human cruelty and human kindness. One is often inclined to conclude that Roa is striving to impose certain messages upon us by sensationalistic means in order to bring the reader to a vivid and more profound understanding than might otherwise be possible with "lower-key" narrative techniques.

Roa Bastos achieves our confrontation with his literary reality by distilling the elements of his narrative to their purest extremes and by then abruptly counterpoising them to create impressive portrayals of man's soul struggling to overcome the animal in him. Biological atavism is the omnipresent menace of the narratives of *El trueno entre las hojas*, and one must admit that Roa's most important single predecessor is probably the Uruguayan writer, Horacio Quiroga. While the "poetic vision" is different and has as its purpose the revelation of different characteristics of the human soul, it is undeniably true that Roa makes use in his stories of the same elements of combined superstition, fantasy, and exaggerated abnormal pshychology. The result is a unity in which the end is not a sum of the parts; nor does the sum of any of the isolated parts result in a homogeneous reality. The product of each of the author's experimental efforts must be considered as one artistic and thematic whole, as seen in the following examination of *El trueno entre las hojas,* which we will call seventeen literary experiments in the definition of a people. [3]

1. "Carpincheros"—THE SETTING OF "EL TRUENO ENTRE LAS HOJAS"

For many and complex reasons, Paraguay is one of the most economically, politically, and culturally retarded countries of Latin America. Hubert Herring has observed that: [4]

---

[3] Two selections are not pertinent to this study: "La gran solución" and "El ojo de la muerte."

[4] Hubert Herring, *A History of Latin America, from the Beginnings to the Present,* 2nd ed. (New York, Alfred A. Knopf, 1962).

In the legends of primitive men who roamed the heart of South America, there was a Garden of Eden a land of lush prairies, thick cedar forests, and broad rivers whose waters promised healing for man's ills. But modern Paraguay scarcely qualifies as a paradise. No country of Latin America has had a more bizarre history, or experienced greater suffering at the hands of domestic tyrants and foreign foes, than Paraguay. After four centuries as colony and free republic, it is still one of the most backward nations of the Western Hemisphere. [...]

Poor, illiterate, and sick, the people of Paraguay offer a melancholy contrast to their prosperous neighbors in Uruguay and Argentina. Their hopes for a free and responsible national existence have been defeated by an inner weakness which has exposed them to dictatorships and continued coercion from without. [...]

Paraguay, an unrealized Garden of Eden, continues to live with the problems that have long plagued her. Her broad acres, especially in the Chaco, are still concentrated in too few hands, while the masses toil for pitiful wages. Her schools, hospitals, and other agencies for mercy and enlightenment are among the most meager of any nation in the Americas. Economically and politically, she is tied to Argentina — still a vassal, just as she has always been (pp. 10-19).

It is against this cultural and social background that Roa builds his narratives, attempting to capture the tragic essence, the "inner weakness" as well as the inner strength of his country's people. [5]

In "Carpincheros," the first selection of *El trueno entre las hojas*, the author exploits the superstition and folklore that are prominent characteristics of the Guaraní people. Making use of what we may call the "mythic mystery," the strange and unexplainable occurrence, the presence of powerful and super- or extra-human forces that determine the course of events, Roa

---

[5] It is not surprising that the present status quo of Paraguay has inspired much literature of protest. One introduction to the artists' reaction against political and social tyranny is William H. Robert, "Paraguayan Poetry of Social Protest," *Kentucky Foreign Language Quarterly*, IX, No. 1 (1962), 45-51.

Bastos seeks to establish a setting that will constitute an underlying motif for the work.[6]

* * *

The *carpincheros*, or *los de los carpinchos* (a South-American rodent, the capybara), are a fierce and nomadic people who inhabit the rivers. Roa refers to them in "El trueno entre las hojas" as the only people not subjugated by the iron grip of exploitation described in that narrative. In "Carpincheros," the author attempts to evoke the clash between primitivism and the encroaching civilization that results inevitably from the influx of new people, in this case a German immigrant family —a man, his wife, and their young daughter, Gretchen— living on the bank of the river where the silent people pass in their canoes. Roa, in a procedure characteristic of this collection, expends great effort and detail in setting the circumstances of the story. Little Gretchen is the center of the narrative. She discovers the *carpincheros*, becomes obsessed with them, and finally throws herself into the river after them to be carried off. Thus, the girl's obsession with the natives is a motivating narrative force. She first becomes aware of them on La Noche de San Juan, Midsummer's night, when the inhabitants of San Juan de Borja send burning rafts down the river in honor of their patron saint. With the rafts come the canoes of the river people:

> Iban silenciosos. Parecían mudos, como si la voz formara apenas parte de su vida errabunda y montaraz. En algún momento levantaron sus caras, tal vez extrañados también de los tres seres de harina que desde lo alto de la barranca verberante los miraban pasar. Alguno que otro perro ladró. Alguna que otra palabra gutural e incomprensible anduvo de uno a otro cachiveo, como un pedazo de lengua atada a un sonido secreto.

---

[6] An excellent introduction to Paraguayan folklore and mythology is Eloy Farina Núñez, "Mitos guaraníes," in his *Conceptos estéticos* (Buenos Aires, Mariano Pastor, 1926), 153-255. The myth which Herring refers to is not discussed specifically by Farina Núñez, but is probably tied up with that of the "Mbaé-Berá-Guazú," the "Ciudad Resplandeciente" (cf. *op. cit.*, pp. 241 ff.).

El agua ardía. El banco de arena era un inmenso carbunclo encendido al rojo vivo. Las sombres de los carpincheros resbalaron velozmente sobre él. Pronto los últimos carpincheros se esfumaron en el recodo del río. Habían aparecido y desaparecido como en una alucinación (p. 12).

These *gitanos del agua* hold the little German immigrant-girl spellbound. Not only is she unable to escape from the momentary vision of them, but, we are told, she begins to find herself gripped by a world of fantasy built around the wonderfully free and excitingly mysterious men of the waters.

The story's lead position in the collection is not without importance, for not only is Roa's technique of great care and detail in creating his settings followed throughout, but, more important, the initial shock of the primitive and almost inhuman atmosphere is carried out in the majority of the selections. One might do well to label it a detached clinicalism, in which the author selects elements conveying a pattern of impressions. In a sort of disjointed style, the writer presents blocks of narrative (rarely dialogue) that in some minimal way contribute to the overall intention.

"Carpincheros" assumes the structure of a series of contrasts in which Gretchen is placed in relief with a primitive mulatto with whom she finally changes places in life when she is carried off by the natives. Thrown into the untamed environment of Paraguay, the little girl begins to respond to her primitive surroundings. The jungle begins to work the same mysterious and horrible change upon the personality of Gretchen that it has worked upon her many literary predecessors who have become lost in its biological imperiousness. Nevertheless, through the mouth of the German, Roa exalts the primitive over the mechanized and social enslavement brought by civilization:[7]

> [...] los peones son como esclavos en la fábrica. Y los carpincheros son libres en el río. Los carpincheros son como las sombras vagabundas de los esclavos cautivos en el ingenio, en los cañaverales, en las máquinas [...]. Hombres prisioneros de otros hombres (p. 13).

---

[7] See also the presence of "industrial civilization" below in the discussions of "El trueno entre las hojas."

The fusion of these opposing elements comes with the despair of the parents over their daughter's flight into the arms of the *carpincheros* and the fury of the native who is left behind, as he attempts to force his way out of the claustrophobic confines of the immigrants' cabin:

> —¡Margaret..., *Gretchen*...!
> Corre hacia la barranca. El hilván de los cachiveos está doblando el codo entre las fogatas. Los destellos muestran todavía por un momento, antes de perderse en las tinieblas, los cabellos de leche de Margaret. Va como una luna chica en uno de los cachiveos negros. [...]
>
> Llega el momento en que el carpinchero muerto [por el tigre] se levanta del catre convertido en un mulato gigantesco. Le oye reír y llorar. Lo ve andar como un ciego, golpeándose contra las paredes. Busca una salida. No la encuentra. La muerte tal vez lo acorrala todavía. Suena su risa. Suenan sus huesos contra la tapia. Suena su llanto quejumbroso. [...]
>
> En el tambor de porongo el redoble rítmico y sordo se va apagando poco a poco, se va haciendo cada vez más lento y tenue. El último se oye apenas como una gota de sangre cayendo sobre el suelo (pp. 23-24).

In order to increase the effectiveness of his portrayal of the fierce elements of nature upon the innocent intruder, Roa evokes the four mythic elements of creation: earth, fire, water, and air. The opening passages quoted above effectively juxtapose these antithetical elements. The fire upon water is a powerful image in creating an atmosphere for the ensuing events. And all four elements combine to create the final violent scene, as the mother sees her daughter disappear in the distance, the irretrievable victim of an atavistic regression:

> Dientes inmensos de tierra, de fuego, de viento, mascan la cuerda de agua del gualambau y le hacen vomitar sus arcadas de trueno caliente sobre la sien de harina de Ilse (p. 24).

* * *

"Carpincheros" sets the background for the narratives which follow, creating a frame of reference for Roa Bastos' definition of the reality of Paraguay. "Carpincheros" is a new approach to the *vorágine* of all-encompassing primitiveness — a primitiveness which extends beyond the mere cruel exigencies of life in the interior to color and taint man's very personality until he seems to work with the destructive forces of the jungle against his fellow man. It is this one theme *(hombres prisioneros de otros hombres)* which Roa Bastos is to develop into the *hijo de hombre* motif that has given him the wide recognition which is his today. It is well to keep in mind as we proceed the quotation which prefaces this collection:

> El trueno cae y se queda entre las hojas. Los animales comen las hojas y se ponen violentos. Los hombres comen los animales y se ponen violentos. La tierra se come a los hombres y empieza a rugir como el trueno (*De una leyenda aborigen*, p. 9).

2. STORIES OF HUMAN SUFFERING

Roa Bastos treats of human misery as a result of the treatment of man by by his fellow men. As the discussion of the novel *Hijo de hombre* points out, since man, and the man-God, are "crucified" and made to suffer by man and by his sins, man therefore is redeemable by man. In discussing the following narratives, we want to consider particular human realities that Roa Bastos sees as pertinent to his definition of Paraguay and of the Paraguayans within the context of damnation and redemption.

* * *

In "El viejo señor obispo," Roa portrays a long-suffering Bishop who was in his youth a brilliant and promising seminarian. However, by his refusal to abandon his Christian principles in the face of the realities of corrupt politics, he is now abandoned and forgotten by all save his housekeeper-sister and a group of leprous beggers with whom he shares nightly his table. Although in many respects the story lacks credibility, is almost too pathetic, it is not to be denied that Roa does effectively describe the setting, principal characters, the Bishop's death, and the funeral given him by the lepers. As such, the author is to be given credit for his scenes constructed with great care and a sense of harmony out of material not intrinsically beautiful. The story is a good example of an exaggerated, poetic aproach which tends to be Roa's weakness.

The author reiterates a profound belief in the necessity for a close contact with humanity, as expressed variously by earthiness, primitivism, and a rejection of those aspects of civilization that bring tyranny and human misery. Thus, out of a personal reaction to religious hypocrisy and as a form of resignation to the inevitable oblivion which his sense of justice brings to him, the Bishop creates his own style of Christianity in Asunción. It is a style of Christian humanitarianism able to cope with the overpowering reality of human suffering and rejection. Cut off from the Church, he supports his colony by selling his possessions, until at his death only his harmonium remains; it is only with the sale of the instrument that the lepers are able to bury him decently. The burial scene is a touching expression of the Bishop's closeness to reality, the fundamental good which his exemplary humanitarianism brought to his people and the promised permanency of his soul in the memory of his dirty, tattered, and diseased human charges:

> Unas mujeres ayudaron a la señorita Teresa a poner el cuerpo del Obispo en el tosco ataúd. Al transportarlo del catre, el solideo rojo se deslizó de la cabeza y cayó al suelo. Pitogüé fue quien lo levantó con sus grandes manos corochas. Lo besó cerrando los ojos y después lo alcanzó a Petrona Cambuchí. Ésta lo besó de la misma manera y lo pasó a Juan Rapai, y éste, después de besarlo igualmente, a otro, y éste a otro y a otro. Así el solideo del Obispo viajó por todas las manos y fue rozado por todos los labios como un luminoso casquete de sangre endurecida, de pensamiento rojo, de espíritu con forma de burbuja de púrpura, pulido por la devoción y el cariño de la gente sencilla, la buena gente del buen Dios, hecho también de tierra y sufrimiento. Después volvió a coronar la cabellera blanca, la cabeza forrada de tenue neblina del Obispo difunto.
>
> Entre todos lo llevaron a enterrar. La tarde dorada pesaba sobre el pobre cajón. La sombra de los árboles. La altísima cúpula del cielo.

Y los pies descalzos del pueblo batían el polvo caminando lentamente junto al viejo amigo muerto que parecía dormido (p. 40).

It would be difficult not to see the Bishop as a Christ figure in the most literal sense of the word.[8] Surrounded by his leprous followers, the outcast Bishop brings to his people a new faith and a new moral and ethic code based on human suffering. Scorned and persecuted, he and his followers represent to Roa Bastos the hard core of spiritual revolution which will shun outside oppression and ignorance. Foreign values are meaningless in dealing with the urgent problems of the present sociological and political circumstances. The Bishop's understanding is met with reverence by those who most need it, the leper-outcasts. The religious significance of the lepers is not easy to ignore. The author takes the greatest advantage of his religious point of reference in the supper scenes. A group of lepers customarily eats with the Bishop and his sister, and the meal on the eve of his death is a frank reminiscence of the Last Supper.[9]

For Roa, religious symbolism provides an ideal medium for his message to his people and to mankind. While speaking in terms that provide an immediate recognition and sense of familiarity (the Passion and Redemption), he is able to put across his particular interpretation of Christ and mankind. In "El viejo señor obispo," he is explicit in his definition of mankind in terms

---

[8] With the influence in literary criticism and literature of Jungian psychology and the doctrine of the "collective unconscious," the Christ figure is being given concentrated attention as a standard symbol in Western literature (if not in universal literature in a modified form as well). The only extended discussion with direct reference to literature that we know of is Edwin M. Moseley, *Pseudonyms of Christ in the Modern Novel, Motifs and Methods* (Pittsburgh, University of Pittsburgh Press, 1962). In Latin-American literature, the area has hardly been touched. Roa Bastos is one out of many in the history of the Latin-American novel to use this symbol for suffering mankind. His many references in *El trueno entre las hojas* and his use of the Christ symbol in *Hijo de hombre* (see Part Two of this study) make it his strongest symbol and insure him a prominent place in any future study of this subject.

[9] The lepers are eleven in number and on one occasion one of them specifically mentions the similarity of their circumstances to that of the twelve apostles: "—Con uno más —dijo una vez Paí Polí, uno de los pordioseros— seríamos doce como los Santos Apóstoles..." (p. 32).

of the lepers: "Eran once, y entre los once juntaban muchos siglos de un oscuro destino, amontonados durante el día en el claro Portal de las Ánimas" (p. 32). He is even more explicit in his definition of Christ, as the Savior of mankind, in terms of the Bishop. Thus, Roa sees his people and his God as: "...la buena gente del Buen Dios, hecho también de tierra y sufrimiento" (p. 40).

* * *

"Galopa en dos tiempos" is one of those stories that derive their impact from the accumulated portrayal of the hopelessness of man's alienation. It is a tale of blind despair, in which a man, returning to a city, takes up with a prostitute only to find that she is the beautiful mistress he left behind, now weary and worn by time and the ravages of her trade. Of particular importance is the suggestion of a society lacking in social communication and where each individual lives a spiritual isolation as intense as total deafness. One manifestaition of isolation and an extreme demonstration of social inarticulateness is the fact that we do not even know the man's name, although it is through his consciousness that the story is told.

We learn that, sensing a futility in human reproduction, the man once violently and cruelly denied his companion a child, thus pushing the woman toward the prostitution in which he returns to find her. As a prostitute, the woman supposedly has the child that the man surprises in the darkened room where he goes with her. It is at that instant that the man realizes who his companion is and flees the cabin. He is found drowned the next morning; the woman is only able to recognize him as her lost customer. The confusion between prostitution and the woman's raw maternal insinct is entirely without pathos. In its naked cruelty, it brings home a twisted concept of life held by these adults — or, rather, one that is in the very blood of the people. It is a twisted concept that springs from the dark shadows of man's soul. The startling cynicism of this story is not a welcome contrast to the possibility of salvation of mankind through his own efforts. Rather, it seems to be an experiment in highlighting the evil latent in that soul. The old argument concerning the necessary bifurcation of God's creation is valid here: if God created Good, then he must also have created Evil — Good cannot exist without Evil in the same sense that a coin cannot have only one side. Therefore, if man's soul possesses bountiful goodness, it must also possess bountiful evil. Between the two, the balance is delicate. If the *obispo* was the personification of goodness and of the author's optimism in the face of human salvation, the stranger is the personification of the evil with which the Christs of mankind must contend:

> Una vez, por ejemplo, [el hombre] escribió: "El peor crimen no es el que termina en un asesinato. Se puede destruir a un ser vivo de muchas maneras. La peor no es la muerte. El peor crimen es aquel al que la víctima sobrevive físicamente".
> Y a continuación relataba la acción de dos chicos que con una ferocidad increíble, con una saña salvaje pero calculada, casi suave, habían reventado los ojos a un gorrión con una espina de naranjo que uno de ellos había extraído del bolsillo. El matiz peculiar de sus notas residía en el intenso tono autobiográfico que él sabía imprimirles.
> Así, aunque él mismo después contaba que había tratado de salvar al pajarillo ("sentía miedo y vergüenza; era algo sagrado que me quemaba las manos..."), la impresión de que él había relatado solamente una aventura de su infancia, no conseguía disiparse (p. 103).[10]

3. Stories of the Evil in Cildren

Related to the theme of the evil potential of men's souls are the three selections "Pirulí," "Cigarrillos 'Máuser'," and "Esos rostros oscuros" which treat of the theme of the evil potential inherent in the souls of children.

* * *

Cruel in its casual tone is the story "Pirulí." Pirulí, sent by his mother on an errand, becomes lost in his boyish fantasies and

---

[10] There is an element of irony in this account, in which the journalist stands in relation to his material (both in perspective and in sympathy) much as does Roa to his own. It is a technical irony which the author is to use as the structural basis for *Hijo de hombre*.

fails to accomplish what he was sent for. In order to avoid his mother's certain wrath, he feigns an accident. His mother is all compassion until she learns that it is no more than deceit, whereupon she strikes the boy in boundless anger. The child appears in a role in which his innocent and impulsive behavior is used to point out and to underline a very bitter truth — in this case, the fact that, in the face of the cruelty of existence, one does not play with reality. The fierce struggle that represents life to this mother must be borne in bitterness with resignation, and any attempt to play with its actuality is an invitation to disaster.

Of special interest as secondary theme are the child's fantasies as they reveal the innocent but still latent evil.[11] The use of children motivated by impulses that they cannot possibly initiate points to a belief in the existence of an original evil, an "original sin":

> El tren de pasajeros pasaba por allí a la caída de la tarde. La gran locomotora negra coronada de humo y arrastrando fragorosamente sus vagones iluminados, siempre había constituido una tentación demasiado fuerte para Pirulí y los suyos. En ese gran monstruo de hierro, de fuego y de rumor viajaba el misterio, lo desconocido, lo prohibido, lo que ellos nunca conocerían. En las ventanillas con luz que pasaban velozmente una tras otra como ráfagas de una pesadilla coloreada, veían caras humanas; las veían reírse y moverse felices, como si se burlaran de ellos que sólo tenían su selva, su estero, sus sabandijas, su desarrapada y miserable libertad en la que estaban cautivos.

---

[11] The disillusionment of contemporary writers in the face of the no longer tenable belief that children are innocent of the evils of mankind is demonstrated in the quantity of new fiction around this theme. One example of the form which this new orientation is taking is the widely read and discussed British novel by William Golding, *Lord of the Flies*, originally published in 1954 and recently made into a motion picture. It is an allegorical tale dealing with the evils inherent in the human mind itself, but frightfully presented in terms of juveniles whose "playing" at society underlines the author's intent. The writings of Spain's Ana María Matute may be also considered exemplary of this trend. Such a trend, while acknowledgeably a result of Freudian *et al.* psychology, should not surprise the critic too much, who must recall that a natural accompaniment to the return of modern writers to Christian symbolism and allegory is a revitalization of the Orthodox Christian belief in the original sin of man.

> Esta vez les tocaba a ellos; se vengarían del monstruo de hierro al que habían puesto en camino un monstruo de carne y de sangre. [...]
> Cuando el tren arrolló a la kuriyú, la rolliza cola escamosa y anillada se levantó como disparada por un resorte y chicoteó en los costados de los vagones proyectando chorros oscuros y hediondos a través de las ventanillas iluminadas. El terror agarrotó en la garganta de los pasajeros un solo y largo grito de angustia, de espanto, de muerte. No parecía un clamor humano sino un chillido de bestias heridas. Pirulí y sus secuaces se estremecieron en sus escondrijos. Sus ojos brillaban como luciérnagas inmóviles y horrorizados entre la maciega (pp. 130-31).

It cannot be emphasized too much that Pirulí's attitude toward the event is unconscious and without moral implications for him. This opinion becomes important when we consider the stories on the theme of human sacrifice, in which the author affirms his belief in the counter-balancing "original impulse to good," or "original grace," which is an equally significant motivating force. The investiture of these values in children (here, evil dis-values; later, values) is a way of attesting to the sub-conscious or unconscious forces which motivate the people, Paraguayans, specifically, human beings, generally, to both their destruction and their salvation. Man thus becomes both his own devil and his own God.

* * *

In the other two stories which may be considered pertinent to our theme, "Cigarrillos 'Máuser'" and "Esos rostros oscuros," Roa Bastos' exaggerated attempt to create narratives of an impressive shock quality unfortunately makes it difficult to treat them in a literary definition of Paraguay based upon artistic verisimilitude. In the first of the two selections, Roa portrays a Negress, a silent and sensuous embodiment of evil, who skillfully works her way into a family as a servant, and then begins an insidious and pernicious seduction of the awakening youth of her employer's son. Her success, if the narrative were more credible, would not only indicate the ease with which the boy allows himself to be overcome by these evil influences, but would also contribute to the sub-theme of the outsider whose influence goes unnoticed to bring sooner or later its terrible destruction.[12] On the other hand, "Esos rostros oscuros" relies for its impact upon the description of a young nymphomaniac. Not only are the descriptions of doubtful taste, but the meaning is obscured in such a way as to cause us to reject the narrative's applicability to our intent here.

4. Stories of Human Will

Despite the unpleasant implications of the foregoing narratives, Roa Bastos is quite explicit in stating that destruction and salvation by no means rest entirely with impulses and motives which man cannot control. In the stories "Mano Cruel" and "Audiencia privada," Roa discusses the importance of will. At this point in our study, we also consider the narrative "El karaguá," whose theme of human will is of a much broader import than that of the first two narratives.

* * *

Mano Cruel is a *pícaro* who makes his stormy and turbulent way through a world which he believes to be his witless inferior, a fact well demonstrated by his dexterity with the course of circumstances. The narrative is a series of incidents told by a poor derelict who sees Mano Cruel in a religious procession, and begins a series of flashback remembrances of the latter's "career":

> En tiempos de su común vagabundaje, Críspulo se había hecho a la idea de un Mano Cruel un poco eterno en su viveza, en su mágico espíritu práctico, en su taimada vocación de rapiña. Eran el color de su temperamento,

---

[12] It is interesting to note Roa Bastos' use of the "outsider" as a subtheme. Individuals who represent outside values and outside points of view appear several times in *El trueno entre las hojas:* the German immigrants in "Carpincheros," the negress in this selection, Harry Way in "El trueno entre las hojas," the "savior" and his daughter, as well as the Polish immigrant, in "El karuguá." In view of what Roa is trying to do, it is not difficult to assess their importance: that of representing pernicious and destructive influences from the outisde which have plagued the Paraguayan people throughout their unfortunate history.

> como el rojo es el color natural de la sangre. Había convertido a aquel compañero de sus antiguas correrías, a ese individuo inusitado y singular, en una generalidad, en una abstracción viviente, sin posible ocaso, como no podía pensar, por ejemplo, en el individuo buitre sino en la especie buitre, invulnerable a los cambios, a la edad, a la muerte (pp. 59-60).

Despite the fact that Mano Cruel is meant to be a prototypic individual, he is still well depicted and is of intrinsic interest. Yet, he is the "especie buitre," the individual of perverse, but nevertheless, strong will who is able to rise above the downtrodden masses. Mano Cruel may not be an admirable individual on the basis of his social values, but one cannot but cautiously admire his fidelity to the self. Among the pitiful lot of the common man, there are those who have the ability to impose their will; those who are able to assert their will for the common good are, on the other hand, indeed scarce.

* * *

The importance of will and the necessity for a complete control of the adult personality are brought home in the somewhat unreal, but still valuable, "Audencia privada."

The *ministro* is visited by an enterprising young engineer whose public works project will benefit thousands of peasants. It is to be executed in the name of the minister, with whom resides the only hope for its success. However, the engineer, a kleptomaniac, is unable to control himself upon seeing the minister's gold *bombilla de mate,* steals it and is caught. Arrested, he is disposed of, and, with him, so is the project.

Although exaggerated in its character delineation, the story ranges as valid opposites the minister, vividly described in all his false friendliness and vulgar officiousness, and the young engineer, who is at the mercy of hands he cannot control. Unfortunately, in his attempt to depict the personalities, the author uses caricature in a narrative whose intent is much more serious:

> —Sí, su proyecto me interesa. Esa obra se va a hacer. La vamos a realizar usted y yo. Usted como autor de la

> idea. Yo como hombre del gobierno. Claro que si el gobierno no se mete, no hay nada que hacer. Queremos que todas las obras de progreso que se hagan, sean fiscales, oficiales. Es nuestra preocupación constante. Por el bienestar y la felicidad del pueblo estamos dispuestos a gastar, a sacrificar cualquier cosa.
> El loro graznó su risa estridente en la percha de bambú. Parecía la carcajada de un enano.
> El ordenanza reapareció con el mate. Los gruesos labios volvieron a chupar sonoramente la bombilla. La voz del ministro se tornó amable, confidencial (p. 64).

However, in the final analysis, the author's intent is an obvious one. The engineer fails because he is unable to exercise full control over his person. The contrastive effect is heightened by the engineer's need *not* to fail in an undertaking that would benefit many of his unfortunate countrymen. Roa's judgment and sentencing are harsh; but until the men with good intentions are able to exercise their will to the exclusion of the tyrants, the *Manos Crueles* and the *ministros* will prevail.

* * *

Related to the theme of the imposition of the will is the story "El karuguá," a tale of religious fanaticism, a "savior," and his effect on his isolated converts. The setting for this narrative of religious "salvation" is again primitive nature:

> Allí reinaba implacable la humedad destructora y creadora, transformando continuamente la muerte en vida y la vida en muerte. Monstruosos torbellinos vegetales de helechos y macizos espinosos que se adensaban en la gelatina negra del barro, como en otra edad geológica; un reino caótico y vibrante de alimañas voraces, de víboras y pájaros de presa, donde no se sabía cómo podían durar unos cuantos seres humanos (p. 112).

Within this atavistic environment, the story describes a religious colony centering around Yvyrá-Kaigüé, the religious "savior" who comes to rescue these people from the degredation of the soul. There is a latent superstition in these people that causes them to accept this demented man's ravings and his promises of salvation through physical contact with him. Like men lost in the desert, they suffer from an intense thirst that can only be assuaged by a religion whose ritual demands match the natural perversion of their geographic environment:

> [...] Quiso que también los hombres, y no solamente las mujeres de su grey, participaran del "toque" de la gracia que sólo él podía impartir. Además de los *coros de vírgenes* (que eran reemplazadas paulatinamente a medida que su irremediable condición se perdía), formó también un selecto grupo de jóvenes apóstoles.
> —Uno por ve y tre vece por semana —me informó sibilinamente la posadera— subía con él al "abujero negro de la luna".
> Los que se negaban a esta "aproximación a la Divinidad" desaparecían en el pantano o sufrían una cura de reposo en la "cárcel" del karuguá. Aparicio Ojeda era en extremo exigente e implacable con sus prosélitos (p. 122).

Not only does this cult respond in kind to the physical environment of the *karuguá*, but it brings political law and order in the person of the individual who can impose this order: *la voluntariosa doctrina*. Aparicio Ojeda admits that he is the vehicle of a transcendent political and religious order:

> [...] Aparicio Ojeda no'hubiera podido enloquecer a todo. Decía que Dio le había encargado arreglar alguna' falla del plan original. "En la creación del mundo, decía Aparicio Ojeda, Dio sólo había pensado en la felicidá de lo' hombre en el cielo. Ahora no quiere que lo' hombre eperen tanto. Quiere que sean felí ya aquí mimo, en ete valle de lágrima. Me ha dado un sitema político completo para conseguir a ustede' eto. Yo ko no soy solamente un salvador religioso sino también un salvador político. Tiene que escucharme todo' ustede y seguirme, si no te queré que un terrible catigo caiga sobre ete pueblo y sobre toda la tierra. Yo traigo a ustede la salvación pero también te traigo el catigo..." Aparicio Ojeda no' quemaba con su'ojo. Ya se hacía llamar Ñandeyara'í [Nuestro pequeño Dios] (p. 120).

The combination of the religious with the political and the presence of the individual who is able to enforce his will, albeit an evil will, makes us wonder at the possibility of examining the story as a satiric parable on the political systems and dictatorships of Paraguay or Latin America in general, dictatorships whose existence is built upon a similar basis of righteousness, or so the populace is told. All autocracies are founded upon the principle of a superior understanding in the hands of the "elect" leaders. From beginning to end, Roa creates an almost allegorically constructed story, in which we have the literal or historical (the way in which the story reads without our interpretational perception), the political or ethical (the direct and pertinent reference to similarly based political systems), and the moral (the theme of the individual will and human responsibility, here perverted in the hands of the twisted religious leader, Aparicio Ojeda). The construction of "El karuguá" is such that 1) we are taken away from a direct social context by the penetration into the religion described above; 2) we enter an isolated community which lived under the rule of Aparicio Ojeda until his downfall; 3) the fanatic tyrant's image is preserved in his daughter who, accompanied by a Polish immigrant, is a high priestess over the tomb (the *karuguá-pantano*) of the dead leader — witness to the supposed man-made God.

Such a story, and such a series of possible interpretations, remove the narrative from a context within our immediate comment upon the society which the author is attempting to portray. Therefore, one is unable to comment upon the actual plausible reality of the series of events described, but must accept them at face value from their author and place them in the context that is the common background of all of the stories. It is a common background that our detailed analysis here is continually attempting to widen. The author employs a familiar technique of superimposing levels of narrative one upon the other, as a series of flashbacks form tangents to the actions in the present. Here and in other narratives, and especially in *Hijo de hombre,* the multi-directioned movement of the narrative technique gives a sense of dynamic process to the structure of the story. The confused and obscured plot-line becomes a fertile memory from which events are selected and recalled to form an impressionistic pattern of reality. The author undertakes to violate the tendency of the human mind to sort reality out into a sigle plane of perception. Rather, the non-sequential approach creates a much-sought-after "subsconscious" reality wherein events are tied to recognizable experiences, points of reference within a greater sphere of mythic meaning and reality. This is the very contribution of the author that we are pursuing throughout this study — his psychiatric analysis of the conscious, sub-conscious, and "ultra"- conscious — the quotidian perception, the base motivation, and the transcendent objective — of the Paraguayan nationality.

5. Stories of Human Sacrifice: Adults

In the preceding series of stories, Roa has dealt with the theme of a self-centered individual who is able to impose his own will for his own benefit, often at the expense of those around him. The role that the individual has in relation to mankind, rather than in relation to himself —his being in reference to the organic tradition of mankind— is more markedly brought out in the series of narratives which we may refer to as stories of "human sacrifice." The narratives introduce the twin motifs of the *hijo de hombre* and salvation through the efforts of mankind. The first two stories deal with adults.

* * *

The key story in the *hijo de hombre* theme is "La excavación." Political in nature, the narrative relates the efforts of a group of political prisoners to escape from the prison in which they are held. They die one by one in the attempt, their tunnel is discovered, and the few remaining are summarily executed. By virtue of the author's effective portrayal of the anxiety and the actual physical oppression first of their incarceration and then the claustrophobia of the tunnel, "La excavación" acquires several distinct levels of meaning. The most obvious is political: the cold, clinical descriptions detail tyranny in all of its spiritual and physical cruelty. A secondary level, subordinate and related to the political one, expresses the futility of human activity in the face of certain failure and extinction. The ethical basis of society is neutralized by the presence of a force or forces, here the entrenched dictatorshps, which prohibit the natural progress and mutual benefit of human aspirations. The intensity of the effort expended in the excavation is completely negated by the prisioners' unfortunate discovery and execution. A third level of interpretation is transcendent; the prisoner's impelling efforts have a meaning beyond their actual circumstances, and iterate universal patterns of the subconscious memory:

> [...] Ella, la tierra, densa e impenetrable, era ahora la que, en el epílogo del duelo mortal comenzado hacía mucho tiempo, lo gastaba a él sin fatiga y lo empezaba a comer aún vivo y caliente. [...] Empezó a recordar.
> Recordó aquella otra mina subterránea en la guerra del Chaco, hacía mucho tiempo. Un tiempo que ahora se le antojaba fabuloso. Lo recordaba, sin embargo, claramente, con todos los detalles. [...]
> El altiplano entero, pétreo y desolado, bajaba arrastrado por la quejumbre de las cuecas; toda una raza hecha de cobre y castigo, desde su plataforma cósmica bajaba hasta el polvo voraz de las trincheras. Y hasta allí bajaban desde los grandes ríos, desde los grandes bosques paraguayos, desde el corazón de su gente también absurda y cruelmente perseguida, las polcas y guaranias, juntándose, hermanándose con aquel otro aliento melodioso que subía desde la muerte. Y así sucedía porque era preciso que gente americana siguiese muriendo, matándose, para que ciertas cosas se expresaran correctamente en términos de estadística y mercado, de trueques y explotaciones correctas, con cifras y números exactos, en boletines de la rapiña internacional (pp. 73-74).

Continuing this procedure of flashback and confusion of the levels of time and reality, Roa stresses the prisoner's sense of the individual single effort as part of a larger one:

> Aquel túnel del Chaco y este túnel que él mismo había sugerido cavar en el suelo de la cárcel, que él personalmente había empezado a cavar y que, por último, sólo a él le había servido de trampa mortal; este túnel y aquél eran el mismo túnel; un único agujero recto y negro con un boquete de entrada pero no de salida. Un agujero negro y recto que a pesar de su rectitud, le había rodeado desde que nació como un círculo subterráneo, irrevocable y fatal. Un túnel que tenía ahora para él cuarenta años, pero que en realidad era mucho más viejo, realmente inmemorial (p. 75).

The tunnel is thus transformed into an eternal symbol. It is a symbol not only for the prisoner, for whom it bespeaks the endless and futile toil of his life, but is representative of the narrative as well and emphasizes the unceasing and seemingly futile collective toil of mankind. Life has been converted into a black and bottomless pit through which man and mankind fall, gesticulating wildly, but accomplishing little. Our perspective, or better, that of the fading senses of the prisoners, is a vantage point half-way down, past which mankind rushes in a seemingly endless and never-changing stream. The suffering individual's conscious perceptions, diminishing rapidly under the pressure of the earth which traps him, become the national conscious perceptions of his people in the personifying effort of the story. Thus, when those making the escape attempt are discovered and executed, it is not only a group of unknown unfortunates who are liquidated, but representatives of a suffering collective identity as well. Despite the tremendous effort expended and, ultimately, wasted, the interest of the journalists invited to examine the discovered tunnel is indifferent, and oblivion reigns as the incident is forgotten.

* * *

The same feeling of despair is left by the narrative "Regreso," a narrative written around the theme of family pride and love for a favorite son. In this case, the political disfavor of the son brings death to him and ruin to the family. The title refers to the return of a brother and a friend, who arrive only in time to witness the "prodigal son's" death at the hands of a firing squad and the mother's pitiful but useless appeals for mercy. Despite the final scene of the story, the pattern of human interaction on the level of the individual (rather than on the political level represented by the firing squad) is an optimistic one based on natural goodness of the human being. This natural good is symbolized by the affection and care of the brother, Lacú, for his friend, Sevo'í:

> Siempre iba a tener ejemplos incomparables en que apoyar su confianza en los otros: el de su madre, el de su hermano Pedro, el de este mismo Sevo'í que tosía a su lado; una pobre cosa sufrida y doliente, harapienta, casi inútil, pero también un ser humano infinitamente

> puro y poderoso en su misma bondad natural. Eso era lo que nada ni nadie, ni siquiera la muerte, iba a poder destruir. Porque lo mejor de cada uno, pensaba en ese momento con los brazos bajo la nuca y los ojos clavados en las fijas estrellas, tiene que reunirse y sobrevivir de alguna manera en lo mejor de los demás a través del temor, del odio, de las dificultades y de la misma muerte... (p. 89).

This is the first explicit statement of the author's basic belief concerning man and mankind: that man individually is good but that man politically is bad. Although it has been implicit elsewhere (e.g., "El viejo señor obispo"), the individual generosity here, as contrasted with the subsequent political cruelty, firmly establishes this motivating reality. The two opposing forces establish not only an ethical conflict that begs solution, but also a positive reason for continuing to create human situations and to evoke the human soul. This conflict represents itself in the form of a mythic thirst, "una sed":

> Desde las guarniciones costeras del Norte, los transportes de carga bajaban abarrotados de prisioneros. El "Manduvirá", en el que viajaban Lacú y Sevo'í, era uno de ellos. Desde donde estaban, podían ver la masa oscura de prisioneros agitándose apelotonados en la bodega y podían oír confusamente los ayes de los heridos y enfermos para los cuales no había, no podía haber, ninguna clase de auxilio. También la sed hacía estragos en ese cargamento humano que había sobrevivido a su derrota para morir lentamente de una muerte diez veces más horrible que la que habían dejado atrás. [...]
> Lacú y Sevo'í sintieron que ese clamor les mordía la carne. ¿Cómo poder ayudar a esos infelices que iban muriendo de sed? (p. 92).

Not only is this thirst an actual physical reality within the narrative framework, but it also assumes symbolic proportions. Thus, the individual characters of these narratives become tokens, representative embodiments of either particular desirable or undesirable personality traits, or embodiments of political themes. At the outset of this study, it was observed that the impressions created by Roa Bastos' writings were such that the individual parts have only an integral relevancy, and are in isolation devoid of meaning. The context, then, is of the greatest importance, and the "human tokens" belong to an organic tradition of which they themselves are not always aware, but which their behavior unmistakably interprets and betrays. Thus, the final paragraphs of "Regreso" move from a portrayal of an individual's death to his importance within the collective tradition of human suffering:

> —¡Disparen aquí, cobardes...! ¡Adiós, mamá...! ¡Viva el Paraguay...!
> Cuando llega a Lacú el grito estentóreo de su hermano, la descarga cerrada del pelotón se anuda a su última palabra. Por un instante todavía ve el pecho desnudo de su hermano, bronceado por la luz creciente del alba. Después lo ve desplomarse como un muñeco, mientras él se precipita hacia el Bajo por entre las hendiduras de la barranca.
> Sólo Sevo'í permanece tranquilo sobre los yuyos con los ojos abiertos, inmóvil y apacible, como si flotara fuera del mundo. Un segundo antes de dispararse por los fusiles del pelotón la descarga también lo ha fulminado a él.
> Tiene los puños cerrados sobre la tosca rojiza. Y su actitud es como si recordara (p. 97).

6. Stories of Human Suffering: Children

That children play a particularly important role in *El trueno entre las hojas* cannot be denied. In this discussion of "Pirulí," we suggested that the use of the innocent child was intended to highlight the instinctive nature of men's actions. This nature is particularly demonstrated by the behavior of children, who are unable to reason out their behavior, and who, therefore, must act from impulse. "Pirulí" suggests that children are bearers of the "bad seed" of mankind. In the following stories, our dicussions will portray children as bearers also of the "good seed."

* * *

"La rogativa" deals with a folkloric superstition. The land and its people are besieged by a long drought. The women and the children and a few of the men as well spend long hours in the village church praying for the rain which does not come. Day after day their prayers are offered up to the Christian God, but in vain. Poilú is one of the youngsters who dutifully accompany their mothers to the church during the long vigil for rain. However, being a young, normal and eager lad, he is intrigued by the "town drunk," Felipe Tavy. Although exhorted by his mother not to frequent the company of one whom she believes to be no more than a "perdido," Poilú enthusiastically absorbs every word spoken by the old man. One day Felipe Tavy explains the causes for the drought:

>Pero el día siguiente, si volvía a preguntarle, le decía:
>—¿La sequía, Poilú?
>—Sí, Celipe. ¿Por qué no hay agua y no'tamo muriento de sed?
>—Porque en el cerro de Kuruzú hay un tigre azul que se tragó toda el agua. Hata que el tigre orine no vamo' a tener ma' agua.
>—¿Y cuándo va a orinar el tigre?
>—Cuando en el plan del arroyo florezca un yasymöröti.
>—Pero allí hay piedra mucho ité por toda parte. ¿Cómo pikó a salir el flor, Celipe?
>Felipe ahuecaba la voz y guiñaba un ojo mirando para todas partes:
>—Hay un abujero en la piedra del plan, frente mimo a mi cueva. Por allí va a crecer el flor de agua.
>—¿Y por qué no te va' a la capilla a rezar con lo'jotro kuera?
>—Na... Yo no soy loco como lo'jotro... No e' allí que hay que apretar la verija al tigre... Dios no etá en la capilla... Allí solamente hay el mal aliento de la' vieja bruja...
>—¿Y ande tonce etá Dio, Celipe?
>Él volvía a ahuecar la voz y a guiñar el ojo:
>—Dio ko etá conmigo en el arroyo... Él me cuenta todo...
>Y Felipe Tavy, semidesnudo, esquelético, con sólo su camisa rotosa que le llegaba hasta las rodillas, su cabellera y su barba blanca, sucia, color ceniza, volvía a seguir su camino apoyando en su bastón de tacuara, envuelto en la aureola cenicienta del polvo. Su aditito de cosas se le movía en la espalda como una joroba (pp. 146-47).

Being the credulous child that he is, Poilú accepts as certain truth what Tavy tells him. With typical childish perversity, the boy forgets the teachings of his mother and his parish priest —those whom he supposedly has the greatest reason to trust— to become enchanted by the superstitious tale told him by the town reprobate. From that moment, the boy is overwhelmed by his people's misery, by their *sed*. In a moment, conventional duties are left aside in careless disregard for organized religion, and, hypnotized in this manner, Poilú sets out to bring to fruition an impulse whose total significance he can only vaguely comprehend. When it is all over, Tavy carries back the mauled body of the boy:

> Felipe Tavy entrega el bulto inerte de Poilú a la madre. Se puede ver sobre la cabeza de la criatura vetas rojizas. Algo explica el anciano loco a la madre, pero ésta no le escucha. Después le escupe en la cara y le golpea con el puño que tiene libre. Felipe Tavy sigue riendo con su risa limpia de arroyo. No tiene otra manera de expresar su extraña felicidad.
> La primera piedra no cae sobre él hasta que Anuncia vuelve adonde están los otros. Entonces los pedregullos caen en diluvio sobre el anciano, y el ruido que hacen al caer sobre él, es el mismo que hacen al caer sobre el polvo, un estampido opaco y sofocado. La suave carcajada parece aún resonar entre el estruendo blando de las piedras. Pero es solamente un recuerdo.
> Tan ardua es la piadosa operación, que todos se secan el sudor de sus frentes. Gruesas gotas. Gruesas gotas chorreantes. Y tan absortos están, que no se han fijado en el cielo del Poniente. No se dan cuenta de que sobre el sudor que mana de adentro, del odio, de la fatiga homicida, están cayendo las primeras gotas de un caliente aguacero. Negros nubarrones avanzan velozmente y oscurecen todo el cielo. El aguacero arrastra a la lluvia. Su olor cercano, su frescura, están llegando en la primera ráfaga. Lloverá toda la noche. Tal vez durante días.
> Después habrá acción de gracias en la capilla de Santa Clara (p. 153).

The old man breaks loose with sardonic laughter when a total comprehension of what he has just witnessed dawns upon him. In a flash he perceives the boy's sacrificial desire, and his uncontrolled spasms of laughter are an ironic comment upon the boy's efforts, for he realizes that the people of the village, in their dulled, witless state, will only see the event as an unfortunate accident. Thus, when he carries the boy in his arms back to his mother, his laughter is a taunt flung in her face. The reaction of the villagers is as much as to be expected: it is as if they unconsciously understood his mockery of them, and they spontaneously "execute" him for what they consciously believe to be his guilt in the little boy's death. However, the boy's sacrifice has brought what he desired, and, as rain begins to fall, the author's final irony is the assurance that there will be thanksgiving upon such a blessed occasion — in the church that represents symbolically the blind ignorance of the people. Was, then, the boy's sacrifice of value? Yes, in so far as it apparently accomplished for the town what was intended: rain and the end of the drought. While the continued stultification of the villagers is lamentable, one remembers that Judeo-Christian tradition in which great works are accomplished by individual sacrifices. The offerings of one person can save an entire people: such is the virtue of charity and the basis of the willingness of all Christs to suffer for the sins of man. Therefore, just as the children of the preceding stories were motivated by an "original impulse to evil," an "original sin," Poilú is motivated by an "original impulse to good," an "original grace" that is a latent charity toward mankind, no matter how stubborn and ignorant mankind may be, that indicates the roots of a salvation for mankind.

* * *

A similar story on the sacrificial theme is "La tumba viva," in which a young girl, Alicia Moral, offers herself up to appease a strange beast, half-man, half-animal. [13] The beast poses a threat to the surrounding countryside and is considered responsible for the disappearance of children of the peasants who work the Moral hacienda. At first, her father is deaf to the pitiful laments of the peons. Their welfare does not immediately concern him, and he takes no action on their behalf. However, his young

---

[13] The *yasy-yateré*, as the beast is called, is discussed by Farina Núñez, *op. cit.*, pp. 181ff. and pp. 212ff.

daughter is more attentive to their pleas, as she hears them discussing the efficaciousness of a cross in confounding the creature:

> "Una cruz al cuello..." Alicia anotó mentalmente este detalle. Ella llevaba al cuello en su cadenilla, junto con el medallón, la cruz de oro que había sido de su madre. Tal vez entonces no había más que salirle al encuentro y pedirle que se fuera. Si no estuviera tan asustada, ella pensó que tal vez se habría atrevido. Esos ocho críos tiraban de ella desde el relato que estaba escuchando; sus pequeñas cabecitas decapitadas y oscuras, sus bracitos ensangrentados tiraban de ella desde los roncos plañidos de sus padres. Ella quizás debería atreverse. El monstruo vería la cruz de oro y huiría bufando con el demonio dentro. Esos desgraciados no tenían una cruz de oro para enfrentarlo. La cruz de pindó tal vez no serviría. Era muy pobre. Por eso el yasy-yateré seguía robando y devorando a sus hijos (p. 183).

When his daughter's disappearance is discovered, Moral is first apprehensive, then worried, then thunderstruck as he becomes aware of the truth: not that his daughter has sacrificed herself (this is known only to her brother, who never reveals his secret), but that she too has been a victim of the very beast which he refused to destroy. However, this awareness leads him neither to despair nor to self-recrimination, but to a cold and ruthless determination to ferret out the cause of his daughter's disappearance. While it is true that the father is motivated by a personal desire for revenge, his purpose is to accomplish indirectly what his daughter meant to effect by her sacrifice. One notes also the motif of an eternal conflict of man with some evil and destructive force of his environment. He lays traps to catch the beast, and is successful:

> En el duelo entablado entre esos dos seres siniestros, no se sabía quién había vencido a quién. El adusto señor del caserón murió poco después.
> Solamente la sonrisa incorruptible de Alicia Moral siguió vagando por el feudo abandonado. Aun entonces la pudimos ver y aspirar en la escarcha perfumada que las ráfagas del verano hacían llover de los naranjos en torno al caserón en ruinas (pp. 186-87).

* * *

The narrative is a flashback and begins with the brother's discovery of his sister's skeleton in a tree some fifteen years after her disappearance. Here, it is easier to answer the question, "of what value was the sacrifice?" The destruction of the beast more than merely restores peace and security to the peasants continually plagued by one disaster after another: little Alicia becomes a guardian angel, as for fifteen years her remains are perched in the tree, the cross still around her neck to ward off further *yasy-yaterés*.

The *yasy-yateré* is defined in the glossary as a "personaje mitológico, representado por un enano rubio que aparece entre los maizales" (p. 226). Half-man and half-beast, his symbolic function as a mythological personification of evil is not to be disregarded. It is therefore fitting that a child should be the downfall of the beast, and that he should finally die from gangrene.

One must bear in mind a very essential observation: that these children who are carriers of the "good seed" and the "bad seed" are, by the nature of their juvenile state, incapable of fully comprehending or, for that matter, of even being aware of their actions. In every case, the six children involved [14] show no awareness of the broader implications of the spontaneous action which they take. Whether they are motivated by "evil" or by "good," they are hypnotically possessed and carry out impulses which come from a source beyond their immediate grasp.

7. Stories of "Man Crucified by Man"

Our attention is now directed toward a final group of stories which, by virtue of the broader scope of their thematic orientation, will be considered as immediately central to Roa's literary definition of Paraguay, not only in terms of *El trueno entre las hojas*, but as well as a direct approximation to the motivating conflict

---

[14] Gretchen ("Carpincheros"), Pirulí, Poilú ("La rogativa"), Alicia Moral ("La tumba viva"), and, of the two narratives excluded from our study, the boy of "Cigarrillos 'Máuser'" and the girl of "Esos rostros oscuros."

of his major work, *Hijo de hombre.* Two selections are pertinent here: "El prisionero" and "El trueno entre las hojas."

* * *

In "El prisionero," Hugo Saldívar is left alone one night during a local uprising to guard a political prisoner, whom he buries up to the waist in a well. The prisoner buried, Saldívar, we assume, goes after food, sleeps, and at daylight recognizes the man whom he has buried as his brother, now dead, consumed alive by ants. The boy commits suicide.

The narrative's technique is the reverse of "El regreso" in that the latter moves from the specific to generalities, while "El prisionero" possesses a perfect symmetry in moving from generalities to the specific and returning to generalities. The principal theme of the story, "man crucified by man," or more particularly, "brother crucified by brother," is introduced in terms of a pagan rite:

> Más que durante los propios combates de la rebelión, al final de ellos el odio escribió sus páginas más atroces. La lucha de facciones degeneró en una bestial orgía de venganzas. El destino de familias enteras quedó sellado por el color de la divisa partidaria del padre o de los hermanos. El trágico turbión asoló cuanto pudo. Era el rito cíclico de la sangre. Las carnívoras divinidades aborígenes habían vuelto a mostrar entre el follaje sus ojos de incendiados; los hombres se reflejaban en ellos como sombras de un viejo sueño elemental. Y las verdes quijadas de piedra trituraban esas sombras huyentes. Un grito en la noche, el inubicable chistido de una lechuza, el silbo de la serpiente en los pajonales, levantaban paredes que los fugitivos no se atrevían a franquear. Estaban encajonados en un embudo siniestro: atrapados entre las automáticas y los máuseres, a la espalda, y el terror flexible y alucinante acechando la fuga. Algunos preferían afrontar a las patrullas gubernistas. Y acabar de una vez (pp. 165-66).

Aside from merely establishing the contextual relevancy of the ensuing events and catastrophes, Roa asserts his convictions concerning the effect of the minor, but just as devastating, local insurrections upon the peasant. Described in terms of a cyclical rite, they come and go without the individual being able to exercise any control over them — come and go as though initiated and directed by hidden and mysteriously potent forces that originate without the consent of man and that seem bent on destroying him. As in "La excavación" and "Regreso," the terrible role they play is not only the destruction of the individual and any sense of the individual's soul, but of the family unit, the common denominator of Latin American society, as well. What is ironic in this is that the insurrections are instigated by the oppressed populace, who, so far, have succeeded only in bringing about their own self-annihilation rather than the elimination of the oppression that is by now as much a part of them as is any other aspect of their individual or national personality. In this way, the wars become terrible human hunts in which man's animal nature is fed, but never sated, by the blood of the rite's victim:

> La caza humana no daba señales de acabar todavía. Peralta estaba irritado, obsedido, por este reducto fantasma que se hallaba enquistado en alguna parte de los esteros y que continuaba escapándosele de las manos (p. 168).

Later, in the pitch blackness of the lonely night, the boy begins to evoke a series of memories, one of which is of his older brother and the latter's importance in Hugo's life. Víctor is considered a godhead by his younger brother, and Hugo inwardly expresses the sentiment that he cannot live without his brother. Yet it is his conditioned indifference toward the political prisoners which he is placed to guard that in the end leads to the terrible death of his brother. Hugo's suicide is but, therefore, the final phase in a cycle of the destruction of the human soul initiated by the social and political conflict in the middle of which Hugo is caught. Blindly and unknowingly he has been the unresisting instrument of Víctor Saldívar's execution. The expressionless face of the dead boy, Hugo, is all that remains when the flimsy mask of life is removed by death, only to show the hollowness of the human form beneath — the man without a soul.[15] Hugo Saldívar's recognition of his brother and the impact of this recognition destroy him completely, both emotionally and physically. When man is led to destroy what he holds highest in his esteem, in this case the boy's brother, a process has begun which will subvert all that is human, all that is the soul of man, and leave him an animal, completely without human expression. The intent of the story is not that of an individual portrayal. "El prisionero," like the rest of the stories in the collection, belongs to a larger frame of reference in which such an advanced state of decay of the human faculties is an actual reality, as demonstrated in the title story, "El trueno entre las hojas."

* * *

"El trueno entre las hojas" is a longer narrative and therefore contains several threads of action. Since the totality of the story rather than its many parts is our primary interest here in establishing its contribution to Roa's central study, we shall consider it only in its broader outlines. Roa Bastos pits two forces against each other: Harry Way, the ruthless Virginia exploiter who comes to own the sugar plantation where the story takes place, and Solano Rojas, a peasant who works on the plantation and who dares to defy the time-honored tradition of exploitation, to win in the end, if only temporarily.

As part of its symbolic setting, the narrative takes up again the theme of civilization and its ruinous effects on Paraguay. The sugar plantation represents the industrial mechanization which has brought the exploitation of human beings. The steel measuring tape, like a snake of evil, measures and plots the land for exploitation: "Los ayudantes [...] empezaron a medir el terreno con una cinta de acero que se enrollaba desde un estuche, semejante a una víbora chata y brillante" (p. 194).

Before the appearance of Harry Way, Simón Bolívar, a Spanish Jew, begins the exploitation. A degenerate and unscrupulous man, his reign of terror is temporary but sows the seeds for the magnificent scenes of cruelty and human destruction that are to

---

[15] See Part Two, section 4 of this study for a more detailed discussion of this theme.

follow under Harry Way, the foreign "entrepreneur." Ironically representative of their exploitation is the product produced. The factory absorbs the raw cane and the raw human ingredients of those who run it, to produce sugar, white, sweet and untouchable by the workers:

> Por fin la fábrica empezó a funcionar. Sus intestinos de hierro y de cobre defecaron un azúcar blanco, más blanco que la arena del Paso. Blanco, dulce y brillante. Los hombres, las mujeres y los niños oscuros de Tebikuary-Costa se asombraron de que una cosa tan amarga como su sudor se hubiese convertido en esos cristalitos de escarcha que parecían bañados de luna, de escamas trituradas de pescado, de agua de rocío, de dulce saliva de lechiguanas.
> —¡Azucá..., azucá mörötï! ¡Ipörä itepa! —clamaron al unísono en voz baja. Algunos tenían húmedos los ojos. Tal vez el reflejo del azúcar. Lo sentían dulce en los labios pero amargo en los ojos donde volvía a ser jugo de lagrimales, arena dulce empapada en lágrimas amargas (p. 198).

Up to this point, the exploitation has been in the hands of a fellow countryman, Simón Bolívar. With the arrival of Harry Way, a reign of terror, inflexible in its iron grip, takes hold of the workers. Life is no longer life, but living hell, as Roa Bastos vividly describes the details of this American's determination to extract the last drop of labor from every single individual under his whip, and then to dispose of the husk. Many suffer, many die, and nature receives them, as welcoming back a strayed one:

> El río era una buena tumba, verde, circulante, sosegada. Recibía a sus hijos muertos y los llevaba sin protestas en sus brazos de agua que los habían mecido al nacer. Poco depués trajo pirañas para que no se pudrieran en largas e inútiles navegaciones (p. 208).

Raw material for the factory's machinery in life, food for carnivorous fish in death, the peasants lead a closed existence that differs from that of a zombie only in their consciousness of their suffering.

The most conscious of the workers is Solano Rojas. Realizing the impossibility of improving the situation of his fellow man without violent measures, Rojas becomes determined to overthrow Harry Way, who is known by the natives as the "Buey Rojo." The battle is a fierce one, with the wild American in full command of the range of power at his disposal. His attempts to subjugate Rojas, who would dare rise in protest against his human exploitation, are symbolic of "man crucified by man." Solano Rojas survives mistreatment by Way and goes into hiding, still determined to bring about the freedom from persecution, exploitation and "crucifixion" of his people. Rojas is motivated by a firm belief in the possibility and the absolute necessity of human charity — the belief that each man is responsible for his fellow men, and that human society —humanity— exists by virtue of man's need and desire to work for his fellow man. Rojas says: "No olviden kená, che ra'y-kuera, que siempre debemo' ayudarno' lo uno a lo' jotro, que siempre debemo' etar unido. El único hermano de verdá que tiene un pobre ko' é' otro pobre. Y junto' todo'nojotro formamo la mano, el puño humilde pero juerte de lo'trabajadore..." (p. 190).

* * *

It is this express belief in the brotherhood of man and in the efficacy of human charity that motivates Solano Rojas to sacrifice his body, to offer it up with his life, if necessary, in the hope that his fellow men will be saved. Solano Rojas is the embodiment of the four "human themes" that we have been pursuing through these stories of man and mankind: human suffering, human will, human sacrifice, and human "crucifixion." Human suffering in the sense that, as a man among men, he partakes of their common lot, the misery and oppression, the social mal-conditions into which he and his countrymen are born. Human will and human sacrifice in the sense that, as stated, he is willing to offer himself up on the ritual altar of his oppressors if it will help his fellow men. Rojas is an adult in full possession of his faculties. He is motivated by impulses which, even if he may not fully comprehend them, he at least is consciously aware of, as opposed to the two children discussed above, Poilú and Alicia Moral. Rojas possesses a strong and firm will that enables him to carry out his convictions. Human "crucifixion" in the sense that, because of his efforts and convictions, he is singled out for afflictions and torments by his oppressors in an intense act of embodiment of their cruelty and inhumanity toward those whom they are exploiting. Harry Way's *poste* and its torture are a cross upon which more than one man, including Solano Rojas, is crucified for his belief in the necessity to save his fellow man.

Because of his careful planning and intense will to succeed, Rojas wins out against the American exploiter. While the worker's revolt and the execution of their oppressor is not too intrinsically incredible, the prosperity of the factory under their management is. However, if we believe that Roa Bastos' intent here is other than just this tale with a happy proletarian ending, we can accept the narrative's resolution at face value: a fervent hope that such a revolt, such an execution of the oppressors, and such a success is not only possible, but inevitable as the realization of a faith in the people and in mankind in general and in their ultimate destiny as human beings. For such a hope, one is willing to wait: "Monta guardia y espera. Y nada hay tan poderoso e invencible como cuando alguien, desde la muerte monta guardia y espera" (p. 218).

Conclusion

With the exception of four narratives, [16] we have considered each of the selections of *El trueno entre las hojas* and fitted it into a scheme of relevancy to the author's mythic vision of Paraguay. This study has pursued a course that would see the individual selections as smaller parts of a whole, and in analyzing the several narratives an attempt has been made to group them according to topical similarlity in order to highlight their thematic unity.

Roa's fictional essays represent, in a way, "seventeen literary experiments in the definition of a people." However, that the

---

[16] "Cigarrillos 'Máuser'," "Esos rostros oscuros," "La gran solución," and "El ojo de la muerte." The first two are briefly mentioned above, section 3.

author's perspective is definitely limited is beyond a doubt. The various stories, when seen as the organic whole that they indeed constitute, draw a picture of the lower strata of Paraguayan society: the Guaraní natives, the poorer elements of European stock, immigrants, ostracized aristocrats. When the influential and powerful are to figure, they are the exploiters, the corrupt and repugnant politicians, the insensible plantation owners. For Roa Bastos, Paraguay is the suffering masses who beg the recognition and the understanding that his book attempts to give them. The author's endeavor is a respectable and worthy one, but at best fragmentary and incomplete. *El trueno entre las hojas* is a tentative program of artistic experimentation, and as such lacks an integrated orientation that its author is to find and maintain in his subsequent fiction. As it stands, the collection is a mood poem which moves not altogether smoothly from the pacesetting "Carpincheros," which establishes the work's total atmosphere, to the concluding title selection. "El trueno entre las hojas" is a coda to the work, bringing together the various themes present in the intervening narratives and unmistakably affirming Roa Bastos' position in the face of what he sees as the reality of the Paraguayan people. There can be little doubt that he sees his people as an oppressed and suffering nation irreconcilably pitted against "them," the outsiders who wield the omnipotent power of total subjection. The reader is never secure in the knowledge of who these outsiders exactly are. Many of them are Paraguayans by nationality, but who, in practicing oppression to serve their own interests, are to be considered excommunicants in the author's sociological canon. Others are the foreign exploiters with which Paraguay has long been plagued. All are seen as allies of forces which would crush the individual and his right to economic and social autonomy. Where the Christ-symbol is applicable, as in the title selection and later in *Hijo de hombre,* the outsiders are the legions of the anti-Christ, the convenient designation for all that is working against what one is working for. And Roa does not blush to have recourse to such a convenient and mechanistic device. As we have indicated in analyzing the various narratives, the artistic attempt extends beyond the immediate present of verisimilitude. *El trueno entre las hojas* is a series of emotional impressions dealing with hidden forces beleaguering an abstract reality, all of which makes an occasional lapse into mechanistic devices and dubious truths somewhat more admissible. One does not want to overrate this pilot work of Roa's, but merely to indicate wherein it does possess intrinsic merit as an attempt to grasp and to define what is indeed an unwieldy body of material, the "collective unconscious" of a people, as well as to underline its applicability to an overall examination of the author's artistic personality. The importance of this collection as an introduction to the work that has made its author important in the Paraguayan and Latin-American novel justifies its detailed examination here. Any artistic failings which as a unified whole it may possess are vitiated by the masterful orientation and realization which Roa accomplishes with the same subject matter in *Hijo de hombre*.

PART TWO

HIJO DE HOMBRE: THE CRUCIFIXION AND UNIVERSAL SUFFERING OF MANKIND

INTRODUCTION

In 1959, the manuscript of Roa Bastos' *Hijo de hombre* successfully won out over 193 other manuscripts to win Editorial Losada's "Concurso Internacional de Narrativa de 1959." In their *Gaceta literaria*,[1] Ed. Losada's reviewer concludes that:

> *Hijo de hombre* se destaca como una excelente novela que une a sus plausibles valores estéticos y al interés intrínseco de su anécdota el mérito de enriquecer el acervo de la literatura americana en lo que tiene de esencialmente militante, interpretando esa militancia como la contracción de un compromiso con la libertad y la dignidad humanas. Es un serio aparte no sólo como interpretación y expresión de la realidad del Paraguay sino como testimonio de gravitación importante para toda América, que aún continúa oscilando sin descanso entre la rebeldía y la opresión, entre el oprobio de sus escarnecedores y la profecía de sus mártires (p. 19).

Overlooking what is a publisher's natural exuberance for a promising title, we note that Roa Bastos has matured considerably as a narrator between the 1953 publication of *El trueno entre las hojas* and the 1959 appearance of *Hijo de hombre*. A unified

---

[1] F. J. H., "*Hijo de hombre* de Augusto Roa Bastos," *Gaceta literaria* (September, 1960), 18-19. Our text is *Hijo de hombre*, 2.ª ed. (Buenos Aires, Losada, 1961).

series of narratives that proceed one from the other, eventually fusing into a homogeneous whole, if not a traditionally structured novel, has been adopted as possibly the best procedure for presenting a theme intended to animate the novel. A rejection of sensational pamphleteering in favor of a cold, clear, and conscious plausibility is a laudable advancement. Thus, the nine extended and often autonomous narratives of the 1959 novel intensify the *hijo de hombre* theme, the theme of "man crucified and saved by man," by means of a logical and chronological series of stories that build one upon the other, in place of the seventeen extremely disparate selections of the 1953 book.

In our concluding remarks to *El trueno entre las hojas*, we noted that the majority of the narratives in that collection dealt with aspects of man and mankind in relation to man's human reality and existence, particularly as demonstrated by Paraguay. In discussing the various selections, greatest emphasis was placed on those narratives dealing with the theme of human sacrifice, and the title story can be seen as the synthesis of a mature theme of human sacrifice crystalized in the person of Solano Rojas. The personality attributes, the permanent ideal of Solano Rojas, comes alive to animate the novel now under consideration. The figure of Cristóbal Jara, who is born and brought to adulthood in the course of the novel, becomes the figure of the individual who dedicates not only his body but his soul as well to the resurrection of mankind. Jara, as will be demonstrated in the course of this discussion, becomes the son of man, the *hijo de hombre*, whose sacrifice through his life and death becomes a vivid allusion to the self-sacrifice of Christ.[2] Two prefatory quotations to the novel affirm the author's intent within not only a Christian-Hebraic tradition, but within an indigenous one as well:

---

[2] Ángel Rama, "Un paraguayo mira al hombre," *Marcha* (August 7, 1959), 22. This study will use repeatedly the term "figure," assuming that this concept with Classical and Medieval origins is valid in this context. We have left for another time the discussion of the figural and typological nature of much modern literature. For an introduction to the concept of figures see Erich Auerbach, "Figura," in his *Scenes from the Drama of European Literature* (New York, Meridian, 1959), pp. 11-76. The general distinction made between figure and allegory is that the former is historically bound and points to an "organic" tradition of mankind, while the allegorical is not historically bound and exists with reference to itself.

Hijo del hombre, tú habitas en medio de casa rebelde... (XII, 2).
...Come tu pan con temblor y bebe tu agua con estremecimiento y con anhelo... (XII, 18).
Y pondré mi rostro contra aquel hombre, y le pondré por señal y por fábula, y yo lo cortaré de entre mi pueblo... (XIV, 8). EZEQUIEL
...He de hacer que la voz vuelva a fluir por los huesos...
Y haré que vuelva a encarnarse el habla...
Después que se pierda este tiempo y un nuevo tiempo amanezca...

HIMNO DE LOS MUERTOS DE LOS GUARANÍES (p. 9) [3]

* * *

Hijo de hombre covers more than a twenty-year period, from somewhere before 1912 to 1936, the period leading up to the Chaco War and the period immediately following it. [4] The various narratives, each with its own viewpoint, are unified by a "manuscript" technique. Roa employs the ancient method of avoiding direct responsibility for his work, while at the same time distancing himself from it, by attributing the work to one Miguel Vera, from whom at the death of the latter he receives the manuscript. Thus, the publication of the book proportedly affirms the universal and transcendental value of a series of stories and memories which on the surface have only a local and anthropological value:

(De una carta de Rosa Monzón)

"... Así concluye el manuscrito de Miguel Vera, un montón de hojas arrugadas y desiguales con el membrete

---

[3] The Paraguayan Hugo Rodríguez Alcalá claims in a personal communication that these verses are a product of Roa Bastos' fertile imagination, as are, we might add, many other details of this novel that on the outside bear the stamp of reality. We have occasion to mention a few other such liberties with historical and physical truth which the author takes in an attempt to raise his narrative to mythic level where verifiable truth and human truth, or unconscious emotions and feelings, are forged into a higher reality intended to represent the "collective unconscious" of the individuals and people involved.

[4] For a discussion of *Hijo de hombre* as an attempt to synthesize Paraguayan history, see Hugo Rodríguez Alcalá, "*Hijo de hombre*, de Roa Bastos y la intrahistoria del Paraguay," *Cuadernos americanos*, CXXI (1963), 221-34.

de la alcaldía, escritas al reverso y hacinadas en una bolsa de cuero. Las había escrito hasta un poco antes de recibir el balazo que se le incrustó en la espina dorsal. La tinta de las últimas páginas estaba fresca; el párrafo final, borroneado a lápiz.

Cuando fuimos a Itapé con el doctor Melgarejo a buscar al herido, encontré la sobada bolsa de campaña. Pendía a la cabecera de su cama, con las hojas dentro. Las traje conmigo, segura de que en ellas se había refugiado la parte más viva de ese hombre ya inmóvil y agónico. Las versiones del accidente resultaron contradictorias; algunos declararon que el tiro se le había escapado a él mismo, mientras limpiaba la pistola; otros, que al chico, a quien el alcalde daba el arma en ocasiones para que jugara. El sumario optó por la primera versión. [...]

Después de los años, en estos momentos en que el país vuelve a estar al borde de la guerra civil entre oprimidos y opresores, me he decidido a exhumar sus papeles y enviárselos, ahora que él "no puede retractarse, ni claudicar, ni ceder...". Los he copiado sin cambiar nada, sin alterar una coma. Sólo he omitido los párrafos que me conciernen personalmente; ellos no interesan a nadie.

Creo que el principal valor de estas historias radica en el testimonio que encierran. Acaso su publicidad ayude, aunque sea en mínima parte, a comprender más que a un hombre, a este pueblo tan calumniado de América, que durante siglos ha oscilado sin descaso entre la rebeldía y la opresión, entre el oprobio de sus escarnecedores y la profecía de sus mártires..." (pp. 227-29).

With the exception of the last paragraph, which is serious and may be read as an epilogue to the novel, the entire passage has strong ironic overtones. In the long paragraph omitted in the above quotation, Miguel Vera is described by Rosa Monzón as an introvert, a sentimentalist, a bit of an aboulic, a pathetic figure who observed the tragedy of his people from the sidelines. One is immediately tempted to make a hasty but not altogether profitless identification between the portrait of Miguel Vera and Roa Bastos. More important is the relevancy of the narrative as established by the superior knowledge of the narrator. This ineffectual man, who actually experiences a romantic euphoria upon the contemplation of his people, their plight, and the possibilities of their salvation, is an interesting comment by the author himself upon his own work. Vera's personality is scarred by the shock which he suffered in the Chaco, rendering his entire mental and emotional, not to mention physical, stability of a dubious equilibrium. However, one recalls the importance of the unconscious drive toward salvation which is supposedly not only characteristic of man, but of certain individuals in particular. Thus, the novel as a whole becomes a personal manuscript of one man whose very chronicle is a reflection of his tortured concern for his fellow man. It is, as Rosa Monzón states, an escape toward desesperation, toward symbols, with the dominating figure of the novel becoming icons in Vera's creed for the salvation of mankind.

Hijo de hombre, while possessing one organic unity of plot, is divided into four parts: the stories, respectively, of Gaspar Mora, Alexis Dubrovsky, and Cristóbal Jara; and the epilogue-narrative whose conclusion has just been quoted.[5]

1. The "Cristo de Itapé" as a Symbol

In the title story, "Hijo de hombre", Roa Bastos introduces not only the legendary background for his novel, but also the inextricably intertwined themes of Christ made man and man made Christ.[6] The ambivalence as to the actual relationship between

---

[5] The publication of *Hijo de hombre* was met with no little acclaim by the literary reviews of Latin America, due in part to the prestigious Losada prize, but also due to the novel's undeniable excellence. A few more notable mentions are María Esther de Miguel, "El libro del que se habla," *Señales* (September, 1960), 12-13; Josefina Pla, "A literatura paraguaia," *Cadernos brasileiros,* IV (1962), 47-48; Josefina Pla, "Augusto Roa Bastos, Hijo de hombre," *Diálogo,* 2.ª época, No. 4 (April, 1962), 14; Tomás Eloy Martínez, "Roa Bastos y la América verdadera," *La nación* (October 2, 1960). Others are mentioned in foregoing and following notes where they have a particular bearing on our discussions. Several articles have appeared describing the recent upsurge of Paraguayan culture, in which Roa Bastos figures prominently: Josefina Pla and Miguel Ángel Fernández, "Aspectos de la cultura paraguaya," *Cuadernos americanos,* CXX (1962), 68-103; Rubén Bariero Saguier, "Speaking of Paraguay: A Survey of Recent Cultural Trends," *Américas,* XIV (February, 1962), 32-36.

[6] See David W. Foster, "The Figure of Christ Crucified as a Narrative Symbol in Roa Bastos' *Hijo de hombre,*" *Books Abroad,* XXXVII (Winter, 1963), 16-20. A general introduction to this theme in Western literature is

Christ and man is central to a complete understanding of the novel, as well as to the universal theme that it pretends to articulate. It would be well to understand this relationship as Roa Bastos outlines it before undertaking a discussion of the novel itself. Referring to a figure of Christ which stands as a landmark of Itapé, Paraguay, the narrator relates that:

> Era un rito áspero, rebelde, primitivo, fermentado en un reniego de insurgencia colectiva, como si el espíritu de la gente se encrespara al olor de la sangre del sacrificio y estallase en ese clamor que no se sabía si era de angustia o de esperanza o de resentimiento, a la hora nona del Viernes de la Pasión.
> Esto nos ha valido a los itapeños el mote de fanáticos y de herejes.
> Pero la gente de aquel tiempo seguía yendo año tras año a desclavar al Cristo y pasearlo por el pueblo como a una víctima a quien debían vengar y no como a un Dios que había querido morir por los hombres.
> Acaso este misterio no cabía en sus simples entendimientos.
> O era Dios y entonces no podía morir. O era hombre, pero entonces su sangre había caído inútilmente sobre las cabezas sin redimirlos, puesto que las cosas sólo habían cambiado para empeorar.
> Quizás no era más que el origen del Cristo del cerrito, lo que había despertado en sus almas esa extraña creencia en un redentor harapiento como ellos, y que como ellos era continuamente burlado, escarnecido y muerto, desde que el mundo era mundo. Una creencia que en sí misma significaba una inversión de la fe, un permanente conato de insurrección (p. 13).

Of primary interest and importance is that the Christ here presented, and here honored and venerated by the Itapeños, is a Christ born of them — born of their suffering and born for their suffering. It is a Christ created by them. The roots of an Itapeñan Christ, however, go much deeper than a mere blend of Christianity and local imagination. Christ is God made man, and by the same token, after the fact, man made God. God is an abstract mystical reality which may exist, but to a hardpressed

---

the already mentioned Edwin M. Moseley's, *Pseudonyms of Christ in the Modern Novel* (Pittsburgh, University of Pittsburgh Press, 1962).

and suffering populace, oppressed and starved to the point of mental dullness and beyond, one does not preach mystic realities. On the other hand, the figure of a God made man, a God willing and able to become incarnate in the miserable flesh of humans, has an appeal that is more than strictly religious. The Christ borne by the people of Itapé through the streets represents the God made man, the flesh and blood figure, incarnated to save them and crucified by fellow men: "a quien debían vengar." The "son of man," the *hijo de hombre,* dies by the hand of man for the sins of man; and it will be and must be a son of man who will remove mankind from the cross upon which he has crucified himself. Let their Christ be accused of being an anthropomorphically created Christ, says Roa in essence, but the son of man who would die for the salvation of these people must be a son of themselves. How their Christ attains this position is the subject of the initial narrative, "Hijo de hombre."

* * *

Our examination of *Hijo de hombre* centers around three personalities which, on the narrative and thematic levels, are of primary importance: Gaspar Mora, Alexis Dubrovsky and Cristóbal Jara. In creating his novel, Roa Bastos has in reality woven their stories, each distinctly separate, into a meaningful pattern. Therefore, it is necessary to see the following outline as an attempt to demonstrate interrelationships which our study will undertake to examine:

I. — Roa Bastos, author
II. A. — Rosa Monzón, MS editor
    B. — Miguel Vera, narrator of the stories of 1-3
1. a. Gaspar Mora, sculptor of the *Cristo de Itapé*
    1. b. Macario Francia, his "biographer"
    1. c. María Rosa, lover (?) of Mora, and guardian of the *Cristo*
2. a. Alexis Dubrovsky, Russian doctor
    2. b. Damiana, Vera's servent, *and*
    2. c. People of Sapukai, including the lepers;
    2. d. María Regalada, gravedigger, *and*
    2. e. Alejo, her son by Dubrovsky

3. a. Cristóbal Jara, *hijo de hombre*
3. b. His parents
3. c. María Regalada (see 2. c.)
3. d. Juana Rosa, redeemed prostitute
3. e. The lepers
3. f. The people of Paraguay

Roman numerals indicate technical levels; capitals, narrative levels. Arabic numerals indicate principal groups of personalities, with small "a" indicating principal personality. The other members of each of the principal groups bear either a thematic or a narrative relationship to the principal personality of that group, as outlined in the subsequent discussions.

We begin our study with an examination of the figure of Gaspar Mora, as revealed in the title story.

A series of flashbacks, the story is that of, first, Macario, and second, through Macario, of the latter's nephew, Gaspar Mora. Macario himself is a town derelict, an old man who is the weak and feeble embodiment of the collective memory of the past. A son of one of the favorites of the dictator Francia, *El Supremo*, his story is therefore of interest in itself. However, of greater importance here is the story he has to tell of the illfated Gaspar Mora. Macario's tale of Mora has every quality of a myth: the old, derelict town "historian" who knows by heart the events that go back many generations, the collective remembrances of a symbolic happening, and finally the ultimate confirmations of the myth, the palpable remains of the *Cristo de Itapé*. Mora's story springs from the unconscious depths of the old man, and is a simple tale.[7] A maker of musical instruments, Mora contracts leprosy, escapes to the woods, lives in isolation, carves himself a figure of Christ, and eventually is found dead, leaving behind only the carving. However, each of these steps implies a larger meaning, a meaning that has been added not only by his

---

[7] One notes that the starting point for Macario's narrative is: "—Fue cuando el cometa [de Halley] estuvo a punto de barrer la tierra con su cola de fuego (p. 18). This phrase appears frequently throughout the book and serves as a definite temporal point of reference, contributing to the mythic network of the events by virtue of the supraterrestrial forces represented by the fabled and awe-inspiring comet.

contemporaries, but by time as well. In the old man's narrative, Mora is the voice of the people. It is he who, through his musical instruments, and especially his guitar, is able to vocalize the deep pathos of their lives:

> Al oscurecer se ponía a tocar la guitarra que estaba fabricando, para probar el sonido, la salud del instrumento...
> De eso me acuerdo. La gente se tumbaba en el pasto a escucharlo. O salía de los ranchos. Hasta el cerrito se escuchaba el sonido. Se escuchaba hasta el río. Me acuerdo de mamá que al oír la distante guitarra se quedaba con los ojos húmedos. Papá llegaba del cañal y trataba de no hacer ruido con las herramientas.
> Aun después de muerto Gaspar en el monte, más de una tarde oímos la guitarra. La voz de Macario se recogía temblona. En el silencio del anochecer en que ondeaban las chispitas azules de los muäs, empezábamos a oír bajito la guitarra que sonaba como enterrada, o como si la memoria del sonido aflorase en nosotros bajo el influjo del viejo (p. 19).

The figure of the *vox populi* who lives the chaste and exemplary life of a monastery monk dedicated to music and charity helps us understand the old man's firm conviction that: "—Gaspar murió virgen...— dijo tan sólo con una tranquila seguridad..." (p. 20). Gaspar Mora as myth is not only a figment of Macario's senility, but a vital reality as well, as seen in his effect on his people, who listen to his guitar with tears in their eyes, as if witnessing a distillation of their agony and pathos in his music. The leprosy that he contracts is equally symbolic. While leprosy is still a virulent and contagious disease that affects many in Latin America, its nature suits well the characterization given Mora. Leprosy is a living death, a disease in which decomposition of the flesh takes place before the horrified eyes of the still-living afflicted. In its conflicting nature, it represents the decay of the flesh while still imprisoning a human soul. Such is the case with Mora. Like the medieval ascetic, the flesh is irrelevant and subordinate to his consciousness, his charity and his music. However, the nature of the disease causes him to flee the village for its own sake. He finds refuge in the backwoods, where he takes up the life of solitude and isolation demanded by the disease of Lazarus.

In his isolation, Mora takes on an added meaning for his growing legendary existence: an incarnation and a bitter living example of not only the physical and emotional isolation of every human being, but, with his disease, the unclean and suffering race that his oppressed people are:

> Macario y sus acompañantes [...] se estrellaron contra la voluntad de aislamiento del enfermo, contra su decisión de permanecer allí hasta el fin.
> —*Omanó vaekué ko-ndoyejhe'ai oikovevandie* [Los muertos no se mezclan con los vivos]... —contaba Macario que les dijo de lejos, impidiéndoles con un gesto que se acercaran. [...]
> Movió la cabeza y los miró desde una profundidad insondable. Era como si un muerto se levantara para testificar sobre lo irrevocable de la muerte.
> Luego, para romper el maligno sortilegio, se sentó sobre el tronco y empezó a preludiar el Campamento Cerro León como una despedida. El himno anónimo de la Guerra Grande surgió al cabo, extrañamente enérgico y marcial, de las cuerdas llenas de nudos.
> —Contra eso no había nada que hacer —dijo Macario.
> Oirían la música como si en realidad brotara de la tierra salvaje y oscura donde fermentaban las inagotables transformaciones. A través de ella también les hablaría, sobre todo a Macario, la voz de innúmeros y anónimos martirizados (pp. 22-23).

It is in this painful isolation that Gaspar Mora carves his figure of Christ. The anthropomorphic implications of this act are here, it seems, of only a secondary nature. Gaspar Mora is doubtlessly well aware of the Christian tradition, and his creation of the figure of Christ is in keeping with the use of images by Christians as reminders of the omnipresence of God and his powers. Macario, in relating the discovery of the Christ and the subsequent discovery of the musician's body, states simply: "—Gaspar no quería estar solo..." (p. 25). The townspeople accept the figure in the spirit in which it was made, as a symbol of the suffering of Christ and the suffering of man, and of the salvation of the soul and of mankind through suffering. Their acceptance is spontaneous and overriding, despite the vociferous and violent objections of the representative of organized religion so bitterly denounced by Roa Bastos, the priest who sees the figure as the work of a heretic ridden by the devil.

Gaspar's message that can only be understood by his fellow man, but not by the priest, is the fraternity of mankind and mankind's common suffering as synthesized by God made man and, like Christ, crucified, as is man in his daily struggle for mere survival. Macario and the people's unconscious awareness of this truth is what causes them to rebel against the authority of the priest. The priest is adamant in refusing to place the figure in the church, and thus Macario and a few of the men construct a cross upon which to mount the figure. The monument becomes famous overnight and the Church finds itself forced to recognize it. The wooden symbol of Mora's suffering comes to outlive him as a representation of him and of his anguish and of the anguish of all mankind as well. He had expressed a desire to leave a part of himself behind, not to die forgotten. This last work of his is a transfiguration of his very soul born on the hill outside Itapé, the *Kuimbaé-Rapé,* the *Camino-del-Hombre:*

> —Porque el hombre, mis hijos —decía repitiendo casi las mismas palabras de Gaspar—, tiene dos nacimientos. Uno al nacer, otro al morir... Muere pero queda vivo en los otros, si ha sido cabal con el prójimo. Y si sabe olvidarse en vida de sí mismo, la tierra come su cuerpo pero no su recuerdo... (p. 33).

Mora's death is not the earthly end of his person. Throughout the novel, the *hijo de hombre* represents Roa's firm belief that there are outstanding individuals driven to find a way of expressing themselves even in death, an expression which, although it may not materially contribute to the welfare of their people, supports them emotionally and spiritually and reinforces their belief in the common brotherhood of a suffering mankind: "—El hombre, mis hijos —nos decía [Macario]—, es como un río. Tiene barranca y orilla. Nace y desemboca en otros ríos. Alguna utilidad debe prestar. Mal río es el que muere en un estero..." (p. 14).

This is the central theme of *Hijo de hombre,* and the novel becomes insistent in its reaffirmation of the necessity for the complete realization and fulfillment of this primordial obligation of man and mankind.

2. Alexis Dubrovsky — The Misconception of a Symbol

The second narrative of the novel, "Madera y carne," is enigmatic in its ambivalence over a realization of the theme and its violent rejection of it. The doctor who mysteriously appears, leads a strange, withdrawn life while at the same time healing and curing the many sick, only to disappear, leaving in a pile of broken idols a demonstration of the shattered ideals of his humanitarianism, functions as a powerful and striking summation of the good and evil which, in a very allegorical sense, struggle for the domination of a man's soul. At the same time, Alexis Dubrovsky is a non-Paraguayan who suffers the distrust and suspicion that is not only common with these people, but with the author as well:

> —¿Qué habrá venido a buscar aquí? —dijo el juez de paz, Climaco Cabañas.
> —Habrá escapado de la revolución de los bolcheviques —dijo el Paí Benítez—. Allá están degollando a los nobles. [...]
> Pero hasta entonces era todo lo que sabían de él. Nada más que eso: un nombre para ellos difícil de pronunciar; la sombra de un hombre quemado por el destino. Lo demás, sospechas, rumores, el polvillo de su hollín que les entraba su basurita en el ojo (pp. 42-43).

"El doctor" partially wins favor in the eyes of the townspeople through his ministry to the sick and his establishment of a leper sanitarium. Roa Bastos draws the lines of his personality well: always silent and mysterious, "la sombra de un hombre quemado por el destino," he seems a being who has renounced earthly life, but who in his bitterness continues to live bodily trapped by it. Even after he has emerged from his shell to assume his medical practice, he succeeds in maintaining a reserve that is more than clinically aloof. His acts of humanity are almost unconscious in their silent performance, as though two souls inhabited the same body: the one, the humane doctor; the other, the frighteningly warped being that María Regalada, an expatient, stumbles upon:

> El Doctor estaba arrodillado en el suelo. De sus manos caía un chorro de monedas de oro y plata que brilla-

ban a los últimos reflejos, formando entre sus piernas un pequeño montón.

Le vio el rostro desencajado. Los ojos celestes estaban turbios, al borde de la capitulación, como la vez en que no pudo salvar a su padre, como otras veces en que también había sido vencido por la muerte.

La rubia cabellera, al ir agachándose sobre el montón de monedas, acabó de taparle por completo la cara. A la muchacha le pareció oír algo semejante a un quejido. Luego de un largo rato lo vio erguirse de nuevo y comenzó a recoger las monedas con los dedos crispados y a embolsarlas en unos trapos viejos, cada vez con mayor rapidez y desesperación.

A su lado estaba volcada la talla del San Ignacio (p. 49).

While one might speak with good reason in psychological terms of schizophrenia, of the split personality, it would be to ignore the essential function of this portrayal. The principal interest does not reside with the creation of either of the personalities. No extended observation is made of the doctor, except in the most cryptic of terms, and only the briefest allusion, quoted above, is accorded the money-hungry maniac of the "ojos turbios" (as opposed to the "ojos celestes"). Rather, it would seem best to speak of the doctor's personality in the most elementary of allegorical terms —the eternal struggle between the forces of good and the forces of evil— "God" and the "Devil." As a representative of the forces of good, the doctor performs his humanitarian acts with a calm but determined reserve, an almost unconscious detachment. Gripped by the forces of his other self, his behavior is on the frenzied brink of a complete mental dissolution. His spasmodic actions are often akin to those of several personalities in the narratives of *El trueno entre las hojas*. The figure of Alexis Dubrovsky constitutes a more normal synthesis of the good and evil present in every human soul, in place of the exaggerated extremes represented by the polar forces incarnated in personages of Roa Bastos' first book. Unfortunately, man, or his soul acting without the advice of his mind and against his will, opts for evil, as is seen in Dubrovsky's symbolic rebellion and flight:

> Comenzó a ir de nuevo al bolicho, a cualquier hora. Bebía caña hasta salir a los tumbos, tembloroso, desgreñado.

> No atendía ya sino a los que llegaban al tabuco con alguna vieja imagen al hombro. Él la sopesaba ávidamente en el aire, los ojos de maníaco hurgueteando las grietas de la talla. Luego la entraba con un nuevo gesto de anticipada decepción en el rostro flaco y demacrado. [...]
> La María Regalada fue la primera en descubrir las imágenes degolladas. No se animó a tocarlas por temor de que sangrasen a través de sus heridas la sangre negra del castigo de Dios.
> Ignora por qué el Doctor ha querido destruirlas a hachazos. No lo supo cuando las vio así por primera vez, la noche de la víspera en que el Doctor iba a desaparecer con el mismo misterio con que llegó.
> Esa noche, borracho, endemoniado, farfullando a borbotones su lengua incompensible, la retuvo con él y la poseyó salvajemente entre las tallas destrozadas.
> Fue la única vez que entró en el rancho, la última noche de su estada en el pueblo.
> No sabe por qué ha sucedido todo eso. No lo supo entonces. Tal vez no lo sabrá nunca (p. 50).

While at the same time the Russian is possessed with an uncontrollable desire to evil, literally *endemoniado,* the one act, the destruction of the idols, appears to be an unconscious realization of a conscious hatred for the figurines that represent not necessarily the people's religious enslavement, but rather their emotional and spiritual stagnation. It is true that the basic reason behind the gathering and smashing of the idols is Dubrovsky's discovery that many of these very idols had served as receptacles for personal wealth during times of unrest (particularly La Guerra Grande of the 1860's). However, in view of the emphasis which Roa places upon the Russian's behavior, it would seem unfortunate to overlook the inviting symbolism of the "ídolos degollados." Dubrovsky's sudden and violent change in behavior is an inherent instability in the face of the moral and ethical demands made upon his person in the form of his self-imposed medical responsibilities. Roa has closely approximated him both to the engineer of "Audiencia privada" and Gretchen of "Carpincheros." The Russian turns out to be the loser in a struggle between forces that would lead him to a secure contribution to a suffering populace and forces that would see him the slave of a monomania inspired by greed. At the same time, Dubrovsky is the outsider who, as we have seen through the narratives of *El trueno entre las hojas*, is incapable of completely understanding the unique demands of this new environment and is as often as not a destructive force.

The best way to see "Madera y carne" as a contribution to the central theme of *Hijo de hombre* is as a representation of a unanimous misunderstanding. The people are never sure of the place that Dubrovsky is to have in their lives, and in view of his subsequent behavior, he is equally unadjusted. The stranger leaves his mark on the people of Sapukai; but, more profoundly, he leaves a mystery and a legend behind that is destined never to be understood by the people. The village returns to normal after his disappearance and it would appear that neither his efforts on their behalf nor his later mania greatly affects the people as a whole. Rather, such a task is left for those who are part of the "collective tradition" of these desolate people and who are able to pursue without faltering the "mission" which they sense to be part of their personality.

* * *

In "Estaciones," the author introduces Miguel Vera, the supposed narrator of the novel, as well as Alexis Dubrovsky, who appears in a flashback describing the circumstances of his arrival in Sapukai. This third narrative unit of *Hijo de hombre* recounts Vera's journey as a young boy away from his home to attend military school. The story of the Russian is but one of the events of the journey. The narrative itself is of importance thematically only in that the events presented represent a part of the Paraguayan panorama so misunderstood by Dubrovsky. Roa introduces along with Vera several details important to the "legendary" nature of the novel. For example, the boy overhears a discussion by several passengers concerning the *Cristo de Itapé* as they pass through this village. He is able to correlate what they have to say with what he has heard from Macario Francia, as told in "Hijo de hombre." Of a secondary importance are the servant girl and her sick son who are accompanying Vera to school. The girl's passive despair in the face of her child's suffering is appropriately pathetic.

The introduction of Alexis Dubrovsky comes when he realizes the sickness of the servant girl's child and apparently attempts to help it. Unable to speak the girl's language, he takes the child. She thinks that he has kidnapped it:

> Damiana lo atropelló con los ojos fuera de las órbitas y le arrancó de los brazos a su hijo. Los hombres se abalanzaron sobre él. Quiso explicar algo, pero no le dieron tiempo o no lo entendieron. No estaban para entender nada. Él estanciero de Kaazapá, que empuñaba el revólver, lo tumbó en el pasillo, de un culatazo.
> Cuando el tren se detuvo ante las ruinas, lo echaron a empujones y a patadas (p. 63).

The doctor begins his stay, described in Chapter II, with ample reason for rancor, disillusionment, and outright hatred for these "ignorant" people. His ineffectualness, and his frustration upon realizing it, derives perhaps from his inability to know these people and the reality of their suffering with any depth. And his being a foreigner probably will prevent him from ever knowing. The two narratives serve as a bitter commentary by the author on those who are non-Paraguayans, "outsiders," and who therefore are incapable of understanding and help. One is forced to return to individuals like Solano Rojas, Gaspar Mora, Macario Francia, Cristóbal Jara — personalities who, as Paraguayans, are in a better position to bring relief and, ultimately, salvation to their fellow men.

3. Cristóbal Jara — The Realization of a Symbol

The third and most significant personality pertinent to a study of *Hijo de hombre* is Cristóbal Jara. Five chapters are dedicated to a detailed portrayal of the one individual most important and central to the novel. Jara becomes an evocation both historical and figurative as a flesh and blood incarnation of the *hijo de hombre*.

The first of these five narratives, "Éxodo," introduces Jara's parents, the circumstances of his birth, and the flight of the three from their unbearable enslavement. The reminiscence of the

Biblical Flight of the Holy Family is obvious. The account is a flashback, with the reader seeing first the escaping family and the background to their escape. Their flight is described in symbolic terms: they represent the human being eternally at the mercy of his environment. It is an environment which is partly responsible for his docile animal passivity on the one hand, and for his bestial and spontaneous expression of revolt on the other:

> Los tres van casi desnudos, embadurnados de arcilla negra. Menos que seres humanos, ya no son sino monigotes de barro cocido que se agitan entre el follaje. Bajo la costra cuarteada, sus cuerpos humean en el húmedo horno de la selva que les va chupando los últimos jugos en la huida sin rumbo. [...] De nuevo parecen animales acosados, embretados en una trampa sin salida (pp. 67-68).

The couple and their newborn infant are accomplishing an unheard-of escape from the plantation where they had gone to work. Many, taking advantage of what appeared to be a good job offer, went only to find that the legend of *Takurú-Pukú*, the *hacienda humana*, was indeed true in every cruel detail. The plantation is one of the many established after the Guerra Grande on land grants from a government which legally condoned the conditions and treatment in these work camps. Roa Bastos sees them as Paraguays in microcosm, their very continued existence bespeaking the little worth and value placed on the human being (note the *hijo de hombre* reference and *Viernes Santo*):

> Takuru-Pukú era, pues, la ciudadela de un país imaginario, amurallado por la grandes selvas del Alto Paraná, por el cinturón de esteros que forman las crecientes, infestados de víboras y fieras, por las altas barrancas de asperón, por el río ancho y turbionado, por los repentinos diluvios que inundan en un momento el bosque y los bañados con torrenteras rojas como sangre. Pero, sobre todo, por la voluntad e impunidad de los habilitados. [...]
> Lo más que había conseguido escapar de Takurú-Pucú [sic] eran los versos de un "compuesto" que a lomo de las guitarras campesinas hablaban de las penurias del mensú, enterrado vivo en las catacumba de los yerbales. El cantor bilingüe y anónimo hablaba de esos hombres que trabajan bajo el látigo todos los días del año y descansaban no más que el Viernes Santo, como descolgados

también ellos un sólo día de su cruz, pero sin resurrección de gloria como el Otro, porque esos cristos descalzos y oscuros morían de verdad irredentos, olvidados. No sólo en los yerbales de la Industrial Paraguaya, sino también en los demás feudos. Enquistados como un cáncer en el riñón forestal de la república, a tres siglos de distancia prolongaban, haciéndolas añorar como idílicas y patriarcales, las delicias del imperio jesuítico.

La voz del mensú se quejaba:

> *Anivé angana, che compañero,*
> *ore korazö reikyti asy...*
> ...No más, no más compañero,
> rompas cruelmente nuestro corazón...
> (pp. 68-69).

* * *

The narrative unfolds the life of Casiano and Natividad Jara on the plantation. One incident upon another, one cruelty multiplied by many, the author builds his terrifying vision of the *país imaginario* that is anything but an imaginary reality to the victims. One would gain nothing here by repeating the step-by-step construction of this picture. Be it enough to say that Roa demonstrates well his identification of the workers as *cristos descalzos*.

However, one incident in their monotonous life of suffering is worth noting, the visit of the *patrón,* míster Thomas:

> A él no lo vieron. Desde la administración a las minas más lejanas se rumoreó el nombre del gringo. En labios de la peonada sonaba igual al nombre del santo patrono de la yerba, que había dejado la huella profunda de su pie en la gruta del cerro de Paraguarí, cuando pasó por Paraguay sembrando la semilla milagrosa de la planta, de esa planta antropófaga, que se alimentaba de sudor y de sangre humana.
> —¡Oú Santo Tomás!
> —¡Oú Paí Zumé!
> Se susurraban unos a otros los mineros bajo los fardos de raído, con un resto de sarcasmo en lo hondo del temor casi mítico que difundía la presencia del gran Tuvichá

extranjero. El patrono legendario de la yerba y el dueño de ahora se llamaban lo mismo (pp. 74-75). [8]

The history of Paraguay is written in the ledgers of foreign exploiters. While the workers of the *yerbal* suffer at the immediate hands of their own countrymen, be they overseers or dictators, there is always the presence of the *gran Tuvichá extranjero*, omnipresent and omnipotent. Inaccessible to the workers who are the source of his prosperity, his domination is nevertheless omnipotent. The foreign exploiter forms parts of a tradition which those who are able must struggle to defeat.

To suggest this struggle, Roa Bastos introduces the concept of the "collective tradition" that unconsciously links generations together. This tradition of Jungian proportions not only passes the human condition from one being to another, but also forms the bond which unmistakably and irrevocably binds one individual to another into one unit. Cristóbal Jara represents this unified concept of mankind, and the part that each must play for the whole:

> Sí, la vida es eso, por muy atrás o muy adelante que se mire, y aún sobre el ciego presente. Una terca llama en el barbacuá de los huesos, esa necesidad de andar un poco más de lo posible, de resistir hasta el fin, de cruzar una raya, un límite, de durar todavía, más allá de toda desesperanza y resignación.
> Ahora Casiano y Natí lo saben sin palabras, entre un anciano muerto y un niño que aún no ha nacido. Ahora también saben por qué su pueblo lejano se llama *Grito*, en guaraní (p. 77).

The motivating forces that drive one generation to build upon another, and one individual to build for a future generation, is explained in terms of this collective tradition. Thus, the birth of the boy is sufficient motivation for the couple to attempt the unheard-of escape from the plantation, and to succeed in the attempt. Their escape returns them more than just figuratively to

---

[8] For a discussion of the legend of the "Santo Sacerdote Blanco," see Eloy Farina Núñez, "Mitos guaraníes," p. 195, 231ff.; in his *Conceptos estéticos* (Buenos Aires, Mariano Pastos, 1926), 153-255.

the world of the living where Roa takes up the personality of Cristóbal Jara to fully characterize it.

* * *

"Hogar" is another transitional narrative like "Estaciones" required by the type of novel with which we are dealing. The theme, having developed along several narrative and chronological levels, demands a drawing together at one central terminal. Here, Jara, the thematic focal point of the novel, and Miguel Vera, the supposed narrator, are brought together. Their meeting is brief and largely unrevealing: Jara presents Vera to his comrades, who, in view of the latter's military training, ask Vera to lead them as a group in their revolutionary attempts. Vera agrees. The short narrative describes the two men's journey through Sapukai to the outskirts of the town where Jara's men await their arrival. The silent journey gives rise to various incidental comments on the part of Vera that are revealing in terms of Vera's personality and in terms of the theme.

We have spoken of the importance of leprosy with reference to Gaspar Mora, and one remembers also that Alexis Dubrovsky's reputation partially rested upon his establishment of a leper sanitorium. In "Hogar," one of Vera's first remarks concerns the landmark constructed by the Russian. Vera is vaguely repulsed by the sight of these unfortunate disease-ridden creatures who are Jara's friends and who call greetings after him. While they are walking toward the outskirts of the city, Vera begins to recall Jara's story. After the escape from the plantation, his family found an abandoned railroad car, set up housekeeping in it, and pushed it across the plain. Vera cannot explain to himself why the car was not missed nor how they were able to carry out their long journey unnoticed, not at least until he recalls the circumstances surrounding their arrival and departure: the great train explosion of Sapukai when the authorities sent a train laden with bombs against insurrectionists. The resulting disaster killed and maimed many, wrecked the railroad and left an indelible scar on the minds and souls of many as one more tragic incident of their plight:

> El espanto y el éxodo, la mortandad que produjo la terrible explosión, dejaron por largo tiempo, como el crá-

ter de las bombas, una desmemoriada atonía, ese vacío de horror o indiferencia que únicamente poco a poco se iría rellenando en el espíritu de la gente, igual que el cráter con tierra.

Sólo así se podía explicar que nadie notara el comienzo del viaje, o que a nadie le importaba ese hecho nimio en sí, aunque incalculable en sus proyecciones, en su significación. La noche del desastre había durado más de dos años. Iba a durar mucho más tiempo aún para la gente de Sapukai, en esa especie de lente, dolorosa, inexplicable ceguera, de estupefacción rencorosa en que se arrincona una mujer violada (p. 103).

Much of what the doctor labeled as passive indifference may be best described, as above, as profound shock. The railroad car, able to make its disappearance only under cover, had, along with its inhabitants, become a myth. As with many incidents which Roa uses to construct his novel, the family becomes a legend whose actual reality no one is willing to state for certain. Rather, it too forms part of the fund of tales in which the people find support for their own state. The most important of Vera's mental ramblings and recollections is the identification of Jara with the main theme of the novel. Recalling again the train incident, he remarks that life has begun to normalize itself again, that many have forgotten the disaster, while others have stored it away in the depths of their mind, along with the other real and imaginary remembrances:

Pero no todos olvidaron ni podían olvidar.

A los dos años de aquella destrozada noche, Casiano Jara y su mujer Natividad volvieron del yerbal con el hijo, cerrando el ciclo de una huída sin tregua. Desde entonces su hogar fue ese vagón lanzado por el estallido al final de una vía muerta, con tanta fuerza, que el vagón siguió andando con ellos, volando según contaban los supersticiosos rumores, de modo que cuando en las listas oficiales Casiano Jara hacía ya dos años que figuraba como muerto, cuando no por las bombas sino con un rasguño de pluma de algún distraído y aburrido furriel lo habían borrado del mundo de los vivos, él empezaba apenas el viaje, resucitado y redivivo, un viaje que duraría años, acompañado por su mujer y por su hijo, tres diminutas hormigas humanas llevando a cuestas esa mole de madera y metal sobre la llanura sedienta y agrietada.

Yo iba caminando tras el último de los tres. Veía sus espaldas agrietadas por las cicatrices. Pero aún así, aún viéndolo moverse como un ser de carne y hueso delante de mis ojos, la historia seguía siendo una historia de fantasmas, increíble y absurda, sólo quizás porque no había concluido todavía (pp. 108-109).

* * *

"Fiesta" sees Jara as criminal, fleeing from the authorities. His plans for revolution have failed through a drunken betrayal by Miguel Vera. Jara now finds himself in hiding in the cemetery tended by María Regalada, former intimate of Alexis Dubrovsky and mother by him of a son.

Again, Roa has constructed a figure of the "living dead." Jara, while not physically dead, is for the time being socially dead, unable to be seen among the living for fear of capture. He sees himself forced to flee society to live in a cemetery with the physically dead. In this way his person assumes a haunting quality no doubt destined to become legendary through this incident as it has become through others. Jara in this episode comes to represent the eternally pursued — those who are born of pain and suffering and who, in pursuit of their human ideals, are destined to be pursued: *cazados a tiros* (p. 117). The author has taken us back to the theme of the "human hunt" so graphically displayed in "El prisionero" of *El trueno entre las hojas*. In "Fiesta," Roa has resorted to a set of circumstances not quite so revolting and has personalized to a great extent the central figure by replacing the merely representative stereotype of Saldívar with a portayal with infinitely greater depth. As in the former case, there is no doubt here either of the politically-oriented intent of the portrayal, and Jara must count himself among the *contrarios*, among the underdogs who are the continual target of the authorities. This man and the woman who now has the responsibility of caring for him form together a legendary pair who represent human suffering born of pain and escape.

María, who appears to have matured visibly since her friendship with the Russian, is the articulator of the purpose of Jara's life and the reason for his residence in her cemetery. She explains to her son, the doctor's son:

>   —Entonces...—bostezó el chico como resignado a lo inevitable—. Seguro entonces que esta noche quiere ganar los cerros del otro lado de las vías...
>   —Sí, che karaí. Él tiene que vivir para cumplir su obligación.
>   —¿Cuál es su obligación, mamita?
>   —Luchar para que esto cambie... Andá a dormir ahora...
>   Alejo se levantó pesado de sueño y fue a tumbarse en su catre.
>   Se durmió en seguida. Había algo de anunciación en ese niño, guarecido en la soledad de su sueño como en una región inaccesible, donde pasado y futuro mezclaban sus fronteras. Engendrado por el estupor, estaba allí sin embargo para testimoniar la inocencia, la incorruptible pureza de la raza humana, puesto que en él todo el tiempo recomenzaba desde el principio (pp. 134-35).

The mother sees in her son new hope, much as Natividad saw new hope in Cristóbal and much as many suffering mothers must see new hope in their sons. Each newborn child is the beginning of life all over again. Here, the discussion takes place as María Regalada is preparing to aid in Jara's escape, and her words and actions convince the child of the importance of their task.

The lepers play an important part as figures in the background to Jara's hiding and attempted escape and living reminders that his status in life is closer to theirs than it is to the sane and healthy. Roa even attempts a bit of ironic pathetic fallacy: "La luna comenzaba a subir su cara leprosa sobre el bañado" (p. 131). It is not strange that the lepers are completely ignored. Not only do the authorities pay no attention to them, but move out of their contagious way. Therefore, they are ideally suited to aid Jara in his escape. It is the night of a splendid military ball:

>   [...] en ese momento un revuelto indescriptible llenó de gritos y corridas el salón, el patio y hasta la aglomeración de los mirones.
>   —¡Los lázaros...!, ¡los lázaros! —se oyó chillar despavoridas a las mujeres.
>   Hubo un desbande vertiginoso que incluyó en sus remolinos a los oficiales, a los soldados, a los músicos. Sólo el arpista continuó tocando, sordo y ciego a lo que ocurría. El capitán Mareco también permaneció parpadeando un instante más en medio de la ululante escapada.

Entonces vio, como en una gran pesadilla, a varias parejas de leprosos bailando grotescamente con sus cuerpos hinchados y roídos a la lívida luz.

En la penumbra de las parraleras, Cristóbal y María Regalada se encontraron bailando entre las cabezas leoninas y los cuerpos deformes. El tufo del vivac estaba desapareciendo, tragado rápidamente por ese otro hedor salvaje y dulzón. Se apretujaron a su alrededor. Acaso Cristóbal distinguió alguna sonrisa de complicidad en las máscaras purulentas que se iban acercando en un ruedo cada vez más pequeño. María Regalada tenía una expresión plácida y misteriosa.

Salieron sin apurarse, protegidos por esa guardia de corps de fantasmas de carne, mientras el arpa seguía tocando vivamente una galopa en el salón desierto (pp. 137-38).

Roa graphically presents his picture of these marginal persons of society whose very marginality is the salvation of one man upon whose salvation so much depends. The image of the "dance of death" is undeniable in these scenes. Taking into consideration the setting, the military ball, bedecked with individuals of importance in gala array set upon and sent shrieking by leprous visions of death, the intention of prophesying doom for these pretentious members of the Paraguayan Belgravia would be hard to overlook.

* * *

In "Destinados," the author introduces the Chaco War (1932-1935) and the significance that it has in his total picture of Paraguay.[9] The narrative is in diary-form, told by Vera in the political isolation resulting from his involvement with Jara. When he is mobilized for the War, the narrative assumes a broader thematic

---

[9] The Chaco War (a border dispute with Bolivia in which Paraguay emerged the victor) produced a large body of memoirs, personal accounts and creative writings. For an analysis of this literature as a whole, see Donald F. Fogelquist, "Paraguayan literature of the Chaco War, *Modern Language Journal*, XXXIII (December, 1949), 603-13. Jorge Campos, "Una novela paraguaya; *Hijo de hombre*," *Insula*, XV, clxviii, 13, introduces the novel in terms of its Chaco orientation.

importance. While the first divisions of the chapter are of interest for the further delineation of Vera, it is at this point better to turn our attention immediately to the theme. Two aspects are of importance here: the evocation of the *Edén maldito* and the War as a *Guerra de la Sed*.

One recalls the ancient myth of the Terrestrial Paradise located in the heart of South America as mentioned by Herring (see above, p. 18). Vera, in his daily mental ramblings, records in his diary his discovery of the myth:

> Creo que en el libro de León Pinelo se afirma y se prueba que el Paraíso Terrenal estuvo situado aquí, en el centro del Nuevo Mundo, en el corazón del continente indio, como un lugar "corpóreo, real y verdadero", y que aquí fue creado el Primer Hombre. Cualesquiera de estos árboles pudieron ser el Árbol de la Vida y el Árbol del Bien y del Mal, y no sería difícil que en la laguna de Isla Po'í se hubieran bañado Adán y Eva, con los ojos deslumbrados aún por las maravillas del primer jardín. Si el cosmógrafo y teólogo de Chuquisaca tuvo razón, éstas serían las cenizas del Edén, incinerado por el Castigo, sobre las cuales los hijos de Caín peregrinan ahora trajeados de kaki y verdeolivo.
> De aquellos lodos salieron estos polvos (p. 160).

Despite the possibilities of this myth, one must remember that Vera is by his own admission an incorrigible romantic and on the verge of shock at the time this passage is written. These reservations aside, the myth still remains as an excellent explanation and point of departure for the whole motivation of the *hijo de hombre*, desirous of redeeming mankind from the ashes of the brutal punishment of God that was, nevertheless, invited by the hand of man. Certainly it is a euphoria on the part of Vera which carries him to the idealization of his fellow men —his fellow nationals— as the quintessence of mankind in genesis, sin, and redemption. Such a euphoria is dangerous, since it is guilty of quickly making ridiculous what is a sublime and noble portrayal of the suffering of man.

A much less euphoric picture is Vera's portrayal of the problem of thirst, which will be linked subsequently with the war. Here of interest is his vision of his homeland's farthest corners, the *Edén maldito:* "En pocos días hemos retrocedido millares de años. Sólo un milagro podría salvarnos. Pero en este rincón de Edén maldito, ningún milagro es posible" (p. 162).

Against this picture of utter despair born of a vision of frightening atavism the Chaco War is presented.[10] It is not difficult to see in Miguel Vera's words, so well chosen in his frenzy, a culmination of the destructive tendencies of a "civilized society against which not only Vera, Jara and others are struggling, but the author as well. The *Guerra de la Sed* seems a final realization of the horror of war and national suicide as outlind in our discussions of "El prisionero" and, above, in "Fiesta":

> [...] ésta va a ser la *Guerra de la Sed...* (p. 152).
> Calor sofocante. Cada partícula de polvo, el aire mismo, parece hincharse en una combustión monstruosa que nos aplasta con un bloque ígneo y transparente. La sed, la *muerte blanca* trajina del bracete con la otra, la *roja*, encapuchadas de polvo. [...] La carne enlatada de la "ración de fierro", no hace sino estimularla de un modo exquisito. Pelotones enteros desertan enloquecidos de la línea de fuego y caen por sorpresa sobre los vehículos aguateros o los esforzados coolíes de las latas. Una pareja de ellos fue despachurrada a bayonetazos a pocos metros de nuestra posición. Hubo que ametrallar a mansalva, por vías de ejemplo, a los cuatreros arrodillados todavía junto a las latas vacías, chupando la sanguaza que se había formado en el atraco. El brindis de Estigarribia ha empezado a cumplirse con admirable precisión (p. 155).

---

[10] Roa Bastos has been criticized for more than one lapse into historical inaccuracy and inverisimilitude in his books, but nowhere as vociferously as in reference to this chapter. In José Justo Prieto, "Entrevista a Gabriel Casaccia y a Augusto Roa Bastos," *Alcor*, 18-19 (August, 1962), 6-8, the author finds himself compelled to answer his critics: "[...] yo diría que sólo he usado libremente esos hechos históricos de acuerdo con las necesidades estructurales o funcionales de mis relatos. Más que la anécdota histórica en sí, me ha interesado su significación intrahistórica; [...] cuando pretendí en "Hijo de hombre" la reconstrucción documental de algunos hechos, como por ejemplo los del sitio de Boquerón, en esa misma Epopeya del Chaco, basados en documentos y testimonios inobjetables, no faltaron voces que me reprocharon una deturpación y deformación de la verdad histórica." Roa adds the following footnote to these comments: "Éste, tal vez, fue uno de los motivos que movió a la censura oficial paraguaya a mutilar la película basada en mi novela, dejándola reducida en la mitad de su metraje, cuando se estrenó en Asunción."

We may suppose that the *sed*, the thirst, is symbolic and represents a longing for the peace and political and social stability which it brings. The Chaco War, which certainly brought no favors to Paraguay, is seen as all wars big or little are seen by the common man: not as a means of righting wrongs, but as a means of destroying mankind. The campaign is a projection of human persecution for Vera — a projection of the oppression of his people onto a much larger and supposedly legal plane. Roa Bastos, through Vera, has more to say concerning the War, in particular the aftereffects, in his concluding narrative, "Ex combatientes." Meanwhile, it is at this point that Vera's diary ends, as he lapses into shock with the vision of the approaching watertruck before his eyes. The whereabouts and the origin of this watertruck serve as the substance of "Misión," the obligation that Jara has survived to fulfill. While the bringing of the water to the front is of only momentary importance, the tremendous necessity of that momentary demand cannot be denied. While one might lament the fact that Jara sacrifices his life to provide that water, its importance as a means of temporary salvation is greatly intensified and made vividly convincing by Vera's accounts that have just been considered.

* * *

In "Misión," the water becomes a symbol that responds to *la sed* in an equivalent role. The baptismal allusion is not lost on the reader, particularly in view of the *bautismo de fuego* that Jara and his men are about to undergo in their long and dangerous journey. The representation of the thirsty combatants and their reaction to the sight of water is very credibly presented in strongly atavistic terms. Yet, the author well understands what motivates these men to their frantic and bestial gropings for life and the water that will sustain it. Despite the seemingly hopeless situation, Jara is driven by the same forces, animated by the same impetus that has caused him to overcome the terrible obstacles in his life. He is fully conscious of the meaning that his life has and of the mission that he senses he is obligated to perform. He is certain in the motivating belief that the salvation of mankind rests with man, either as a vehicle of God or as the initiator himself of the task:

80 THE MYTH OF PARAGUAY

>—¿Crees en el milagro, Cristóbal?
>—¿Milagro?
>—Que ocurra algo imposible. Eso que sólo Dios puede hacer...
>—Lo que no puede hacer el hombre, nadie más puede hacer—dijo él ásperamente.
>—Sí... Tal vez eso es la fuerza que hace los milagros.
>—No sé. No entiendo lo que se dice con palabras. Sólo entiendo lo que soy capaz de hacer. Tengo una misión. Voy a cumplirla. Eso es lo que entiendo (p. 199).

There is nothing epic about the figure of Jara, as his dialogue with the woman reveals. His function is not to fulfill the role of a superhero who will save his people. Rather — and of this he is aware — he must be one responsible individual among countless many who will, working together, effect some good. It is important to remember that in the novel, Jara is the figure of the *hijo de hombre only* in that he represents many who fulfill a role analogous to his. Thus he is not an allegorical entity that would of necessity embody *all* of the traits and synthesize all of the aspects of those of which, in reality, he is only a single and very mortal representative. It is necesary to keep in mind the collective tradition that binds men to mankind, and not to see Jara as either a superman or a superhero. Perhaps for this reason his ultimate task, his "mission to fulfill" is a very insignificant one in the long run. Still, for the majority of mankind, insignificance and oblivion are its lot, and not heroic martyrdom:

> [...] Pero, de pronto, en su descuido, estaban otra vez ahí, profundos, borrosos, zahoríes, inventando el camino, empujando la marcha. Porque ahora no había más que avanzar, avanzar siempre, avanzar a toda costa, a través de la selva, del desierto, de los elementos desencadenados, de la cabeza muerta de un amigo, a través de ese trémolo en que vida y muerte se juntaban sobre un límite imprecisable. Eso era el destino. Y qué podía ser el destino para un hombre como Cristóbal Jara, sino conducir su obsesión como un esclavo por un angosto pique en la selva o por la llanura infinita, colmada con el salvaje olor de la libertad. Ir abriéndose paso en la inexorable maraña de los hechos, dejando la carne en ella, pero transformándolos también con el elemento de esa voluntad cuya fuerza crecía precisamente al integrase en ellos. *Lo que no puede hacer el*

hombre, nadie más puede hacerlo..., había dicho él mismo. Y había muchos como él, incontables, anónimos. No estribaba acaso su fuerza en la simplicidad de atacar una ley que los incluía y los sobrepasaba. No sabían nada, ni siquiera tal vez lo que es la esperanza. Nada más que eso: querer algo hasta olvidar todo lo demás. Seguir adelante, olvidándose de sí mismos. Alegría, triunfo, derrota, sexo, amor, desesperación, no eran más que eso: tramos de la marcha por un desierto sin límites. Uno caía, otro seguía adelante, dejando un surco, una huella, un rastro de sangre, sobre la vieja costra, pero entonces la feroz y elemental virginidad quedaba fecundada (p. 201).

Roa bastos makes it explicitly clear that he is not attempting to construct a narrative of impressive heroics; he is attempting to express the *realidad histórica* of Paraguay common not only to the Paraguayan people, not only to the Latin-American common man, but to the majority of mankind everywhere. What makes the monotony of life of any transcendent importance is the altruism of a few like Jara who, while they may not be able to change the monotony and insignificance of day-to-day living, may at least change it from an oblivion of physical torment. The Chaco War, an actual reality, is at the same time also a figure of this life of struggle — "tramos de la marcha por un desierto sin límites". Jara does not survive the War, but others do, and Roa's final offering in the development of his novel is "Ex combatientes."

4. "Ex combatientes" — The Legacy of a Symbol

Vera assumes in this final narrative a very marginal role: Roa Bastos succeeds in creating through the former's story the impression of loneliness and social isolation. The isolation, sensed by the reader, is confirmed in the closing passages of the novel, consisting of the letter of transmittal accompanying the manuscript, and indicates a "sentencing" of Vera to oblivion because of his failure to play an active role. However, these considerations are only secondary. More important, "Ex combatientes" presents three aspects of our theme as seen through Vera's narrative: 1) the figure of the hollow man, a result of the War; 2) the execution and crucifixion in the place of man of the political leader for his corruption; and 3) a final affirmation of the still unsatisfied *sed* of the people.

Vera first presents us with a moving picture of the let-down which normally follows war. The entire citizenry suddenly sees the only reason for its existence abolished by a few signatures on a peace treaty. Confused ond bewildered, the participants are usually unable to make the transition from front-line trench to human society without outside assistance. The impact of such a radical transition often results in an emotional state similar to that of this "returning hero":

> Echó a andar con lentitud. El polvo se enroscó a la escuálida figura del ex combatiente. Subió hasta la picuda cara de pájaro donde la piel reseca se pegaba al hueso, curtida, grabada a fuego por los espinos del Chaco, por los gránulos morados y apagados de la pólvora que le embijaban los pómulos terrosos, uno de ellos arado a quemarropa por el tajo de una bala (p. 205-206).
> —¡Tres hurras al valiente hijo del pueblo, al invicto sargento Jocó!—volvió a gritar Corazón, entusiasmado con el éxito—. ¡Hip..., hip..., hip!...
> Se había juntado mucha gente. La pequeña multitud vitoreó con un entusiasmo un poco falso. Yo sentía que mis gritos trataban de exaltar no al ex combatiente del Chaco, sino a esa triste sombra parada en la luz cenital, la escueta, la indomable sombra de un hombre (p. 209).

Vera senses the falseness of the situation. There is nothing false in the people's willingness to honor the hero; what is false is his status as a hero. He is crushed and beaten by the war —of this there is no doubt— and therefore does not really want their adulations. The end result is a universal hypocrisy, as the same scene is enacted in town after town.

The man is a living representative of the emotional ravages of the War. [11] He is seen as the shell of a human being who

---

[11] In the same interview Prieto quoted above, Roa goes on to say that: "Bien, pero lo que a mí me interesaba como novelista, por encima de esos tiros mal reglados de la artillería y los fusilamientos de los desertores, era en sí mismo el trágico absurdo de esa guerra entre dos pueblos hermanos, las causas o motivaciones de aquel entuerto histórico.

openly and frankly admits that demobilization and discharge for him were not welcome and for whom the only meaning in life was phrased in terms of the War which is now history. Jocó's letdown is felt on all levels of the narrative: by the narrator, Miguel Vera, who evokes the pitiful figure of the hollow man, sustained by no moral or ethical conviction of his own, but hero according to the false, empty principles of an untenable policy; by the man himself, whose actions and speech betray the profound state of shock of which he is victim; and by the reader, whose feeling of hopeless despair attests to the power of the portrayal. The same emotional vacuum has been achieved in "Galopa en dos tiempos" of *El trueno entre las hojas* on a personal level.

* * *

Nevertheless, not all return with the beaten attitude of Jocó. Others are openly infuriated with their leaders, and return for vengeance:

> A su regreso del Chaco, los mellizos Goiburú ajusticiaron a Melitón Isasi, de la terrible manera cuyo remate todo el pueblo descubrió consternado al día siguiente, en un escarmiento de impar ferocidad, condigno de la culpa, pero cuyo sentido sobrepasaba la simple enormidad del dolor o del odio. Ejecutaron al jefe político, saldando a un tiempo su venganza con el corruptor de su hermana y también la vieja deuda de descreimiento y encono que tenían con el Cristo. Por eso los itapeños tardaron en entender la acción de los Goiburú. Tardaron en comprender por qué, arrancando al Cristo de la cruz, ataron a ella en su lugar, con varias vueltas de lazo, al jefe político ya emasculado y muerto, como si en un cuarto de siglo de estar colgado allí, al aire libre, al amor de los vientos, de los pájaros, del sol y de las lluvias, y no en la penumbra rancia a incienso aromático de la iglesia, también el Cristo de Gaspar Mora hubiera amanecido de repente una mañana vestido de jefe político, campera, botas, pistolera y esa cara fofa de ojos inyectados en sangre, sobre la cual las sombras de los yrybúes ya empezaron a revolar (pp. 214-15).

While at the same time the brothers' act is a profanation of the Cristo, it is also a crucifixion of the political boss who had so oppressed them and their fellow citizens. Their act is as if they had replaced the figure of persecuted mankind with the figure of the persecutors upon the cross symbolic of man's burden. On the other hand, it is not explicitly clear how much of what they do is a symbolic profanation of the Cristo; i.e., how broadly their personal grudge against it is to be interpreted. In any case, there is the strong suggestion of a desecration of the popular image as well as the crucifixion of the political leader. If the Cristo was created by a hopeful populace, it can equally be destroyed by a disillusioned one.

That the people have ample reason for disillusionment is also a concern of Vera at this point. The reader must remind himself that Vera's principal virtue is that he is agonizingly aware of the plight of his fellow Paraguayans. Indeed, the novel supposedly owes its existence to this awareness. The soldier is well acquainted with all of the types developed in the novel — from the tender, artistic individuality of Gaspar Mora to the strident virility of Cristóbal Jara on the one hand, from the sickening resignation of Damiana to the homicidal fury of the brothers Goiburú on the other. We quote the following passage of his concluding account, for in it Vera demonstrates, despairingly yet prophetically, the continued unfulfillment of the *sed*, his people's desire to be human beings in the fullest sense of the word:

> [...] Yo sigo, pues, viviendo, a mi modo, más interesado en lo que he visto que en lo que aún me queda por ver. [...] Pero para estos hombres sólo cuenta el futuro, que debe tener una antigüedad tan fascinadora como la del pasado. No piensan en la muerte. Se sienten vivir en los hechos. Se sienten unidos en la pasión del instante que los proyecta fuera de sí mismos, ligándolos a una causa verdadera o engañosa, pero a algo... No hay otra vida para ellos. No existe la muerte. Pensar en ella es lo que corroe y mata. Ellos viven, simplemente. Aun el extravío de Cristiano Villalba es una pasión devoradora como la vida. La aguja de la sed marca para ellos la dirección del agua en el desierto, el más misterioso, sediento e ilimitado de todos: el corazón humano. La fuerza de su indestructible fraternidad es su Dios. La aplastan, la rompen, la desmenuzan, pero vuelve a recomponerse de los fragmentos, cada vez más viva y pujante. Y sus ciclos se expanden en espiral. [...]

Algo tiene que cambiar. No se puede seguir oprimiendo a un pueblo indefinidamente. El hombre es como un río, mis hijos..., decía el viejito Macario Francia. Nace y muere en otros ríos. Mal río es el que muere en un estero... El agua estancada es ponzoñosa. Engendra miasmas de una fiebre maligna, de una furiosa locura. luego, para curar al enfermo o apaciguarlo, hay que matarlo. Y el suelo de este país ya está bastante ocupado bajo tierra. "¡Los muertos bajo la tierra no prenden!..."

Temo que un día de éstos vengan a proponerme, como allá en Sapukai, que les enseñe a combatir. ¡Yo a ellos..., qué escarnio! Pero no, ya no lo necesitan. Han aprendido mucho. El camión de Cristóbal Jara no atravesó la muerte para salvar la vida de un traidor. Envuelto en llamas sigue rodando en la noche, sobre el desierto, en las picadas, llevando el agua para la sed de los sobrevivientes. [...]

A lo lejos, sobre la carretera parpadeante de opacos destellos, se desvanecían las nubecitas de polvo que habían levantado los pasos de Crisanto y de su hijo (pp. 222-23).

* * *

Roa Bastos has employed a diffuse technique to construct his novel. Not only does this technique result in a wide panorama of events and personalities, but prevents the stagnation of the thematic economy which he is attempting to execute. At the same time, he has succeeded in presenting a sweeping analysis not only of the collective tradition of his country in terms of the representative and figurative *hijo de hombre,* but has as well spoken in terms applicable to all mankind. He has seen, in the course of unfolding his novel, the appearance of the *Cristo de Itapé,* the verification on both a personal and a collective level of the necessity for its existence, the reaffirmation of his people's suffering by the representation of the Chaco War, the lost existence of mankind in the face of war and oppression, and the sowing of the seeds of an earnest revolt and an ultimate progress. He has expressed his firm conviction that man cannot and will not continue to sanction his own martyrdom and crucifixion and has stated explicitly his sincere belief that the salvation of mankind will be effected by a responsible body of individuals who will have as their goal the ultimate realization of the term *human being*. In the words of Vera, "la fuerza de su indestructible fraternidad es su Dios."

Conclusion

The final pages of *Hijo de hombre* represent Roa's most significant prose fiction to the date of this writing.[12] Perhaps it is difficult —possibly even dangerous— to generalize the importance of an author from what appears to be a scant body of writings, and at that only a promising beginning. Yet, Augusto Roa Bastos has achieved for himself such a wide reading public and has won such wide acclaim internationally that he has already attained a secure foothold as one of the best in that most fertile field of the Latin-American novel. Even his bitter and barbed attacks on his own people and the political and social structure of Paraguay have done little to dim his popularity among the young and perceptive intelligentsia of that country, and have probably helped to increase it.[13] Roa's work stands on its own merits, and his thematic intent is obvious enough to preclude any extensive summary at this point. We hope that our analysis has elucidated the path which Roa sees his symbols taking.

---

[12] Roa is completing at the moment the new novel which his reading public so eagerly awaits. It will be published by Sudamericana in Buenos Aires. The recent collection, *El baldío* (Buenos Aires, Losada, 1967), brings together several scattered and minor pieces. *Los pies sobre el agua* (Buenos Aires, Centro Editor de América Latina, 1967), with one exception, reproduces narratives discussed in this study.

[13] In a U. S. State Department-sponsored visit to the University of Washington campus, October 3, 1963, Miss Josefina Pla, poetess, ceramicist and cultural spokesman for Paraguay, presented a lecture on Paraguayan literature and culture in which she accorded a high place to Roa Bastos. In aswer to several questions concerning Roa and contemporary Paraguayan letters, Miss Pla remarked that despite the fact that Roa's work has been prohibited on occasion and the fact that many of his fictional observations have wounded the overweening national pride of many Paraguayans, his work is avidly read and discussed by the young intellectuals. Roa appears to be the most outspoken and angriest of the young men of Paraguayan origin writing today. It is worth noting, however, that Roa, as are many "enemies" of the Stroessner regime, is free to come and go at will in Paraguay.

Roa conceives of mankind in terms of one organic and spiritual evolution striving toward its fulfillment. Many of the stories of *El trueno entre las hojas* and the entire basis of *Hijo de hombre* constitute the mostly unconscious reaction of man to the social necessities of his fellow beings. Cristóbal Jara is seen as a link in a chain of evolution extending back through his parents to the founder of Sapukai and forward by Vera toward the fulfillment of his people. Indeed, the structure of *Hijo de hombre* points to a mythic concept of history in which the present merges with the past to foreshadow the future. The novel runs the range of the historical formation of the Paraguayan people from Dr. Francia to the present day and in so doing points to a criterion of examination within this context, as we have attempted to do. Thus, despite the inviting tendency to do so, the various symbolic personalities cannot be seen as allegorical figures without doing violence to this inherent structure. Allegory implies an overview in which the figures absorb up into themselves a total and therefore non-individual perspective of human emotion. The result is a stereotyped person unreal and impossible in himself and unable to function credibly in the usual human environment. In Roa's work, in particular in the novel, the important figures rise up out of the vital mainstream of human existence as indicative and analogous of a whole, but by no means as as synthesis of that whole. They always remain historically bound, no matter how important they may become thematically. The narrative concentrates its attention on an individual in order to speak always on a human level and not just in the abstract terms of all humanity. The individuals chosen for narrative highlighting are of only relative importance, as each in turn fulfills his "task" and sinks back into the current of life. But mankinds is always the better for the efforts of these individuals, and this is the key not only to Vera's prophetic vision but to their pertinency to humanity as well.

More than merely having forged a series of narratives which capture the spirit of Paraguayan social history, Roa's work, as it evolves throught the experimental techniques and orientations of *El trueno entre las hojas*, has created a prophetic vision of mankind as a continuing struggle of self-liberation and self-progression toward the ultimate resolution of a vital and sensitive human fraternity. Roa's fiction is no isolated phenomenon. Although it is perhaps surprising that one of the most important works of fiction in 20th-century Latin-American letters should come out of culturally starved Paraguay, its orientation and its perspective that successively embrace individual, national, and ultimately, universal levels of interpretation is sympathetic to the broad trends of Latin-American fiction today.[14] For these cultural reasons, for these literary reasons, and, above all, for these human reasons, we feel that Augusto Roa Bastos is one of the most important and exciting novelists writing today and have thus dedicated this study to his work.

---

[14] It would be impossible to mention all of the Latin-American novelists of promise writing today who use the same "mythic and socio-cultural" techniques of Roa. A few which come immediately to mind are Mexico's Juan Rulfo, Agustín Yáñez; Argentina's Ernesto Sábato; Colombia's Gabriel García Márquez; Brazil's Adonias Filho; and, in a different and more metaphysical sense, Cuba's Alejo Carpentier.

The Department of Romance Studies Digital Arts and Collaboration Lab at the University of North Carolina at Chapel Hill is proud to support the digitization of the North Carolina Studies in the Romance Languages and Literatures series.

www.ingramcontent.com/pod-product-compliance
Lightning Source LLC
Chambersburg PA
CBHW020422230426
43663CB00007BA/1270